ONE
FINAL
PASS

D0556569

ARTHUR L. LINDSAY WITH JAN BERRINGER
FOREWORD BY RON BROWN

ONE FINAL PASS

Arthur L. Lindsay, One Final Pass

ISBN 978-0-9845750-4-6

Cross Training Publishing
P.O. Box 1874
Kearney, NE 68848
(308) 293-3891

This book is manufactured in the United States of America.

Library of Congress Cataloging in Publication Data in Progress.

DEDICATION

The Brook Berringer Story 15 Years Later is dedicated to all the
recipients of the Brook Berringer Scholarship
and to those who have qualified to be named to the
Brook Berringer Citizenship Team.

And to all of Brook's incredible nieces and nephews.

Brook's nephews Tyson and Colton,
the biggest little Husker fans ever.

ABOUT THE AUTHORS

Jan Berringer is the mother of Nicoel, Brook, and Drue Berringer and is an elementary school teacher in Goodland, Kansas.

Arthur L. Lindsay is active as a public speaker, having spoken in ten countries on four continents. He is the father of four: Tedrin, Timothy, Linda and Colin.

Art has been a resident of Lincoln, Nebraska since 1988. Though he has many interests, his primary focus is on his own personal relationship with Jesus Christ. Therefore, he steadily studies and memorizes the Word of God. Second to that he loves to share his faith with men in one-on-one discipleship training. Additionally he has been involved in prison ministry for nearly fifty-five years.

He is the author of twelve previous books. Four of them are biographies: *I Can, Coach Ron Brown's Search for Success; Not Even a Thread: When a rapist repents …God; One Final Pass: the Brook Berringer Story; and I Can 2.*, There have been five histories, the first four written by request: *It Takes a Home: Commemorating 90 year of service of People's City Mission; Most Unusual Packages, the story of Bethphage; Influence, a history of the Nebraska Fellowship of Christian Athletes; A Tree Grows in Lincoln, a history of Christ Temple Church;* and *The Diary, a World War Two hero story.* Art has also written a novel, *Three Wings Against the Monkey;* and two books on ethics for the insurance industry: *Don't Punt* and *Cover All the Bases.*

TABLE OF CONTENTS

	Foreword by Ron Brown	7
	Introduction by Jan Berringer	9
	Prologue	15
1.	Father/Son	17
2.	Time to Swim	25
3.	Refocus on Football	33
4.	Three Years in the Shadows	43
5.	Thrust Into the Limelight	51
6.	Quarterback Controversy	59
7.	Orange Bowl 1994–A Championship	63
8.	Hopes for 1995	69
9.	Disappointment and Gain	77
10.	Greatest Season of All	87
11.	Book Berringer Day	93
12.	Never a Dull Moment	99
13.	Watching from the Sidelines	105
14.	Graduation	111
15.	Fiesta Bowl	115
16.	The Hula Bowl & The NFL	123
17.	Nationwide Demand	129
18.	Senior Basketball	133
19.	A Final Touch-and-Go	137
20.	In Lasting Honor	151
	Epilogue	161
15 Years Later...		
	In Jan's Words	169
	Reflections on Brook	179
	Tributes Worthy of the Man	189
	Brook Berringer Citizenship Team	197

FOREWORD BY RON BROWN

I n many ways, it's easy for me to revisit Brook Berringer's life 15 years later. What comes first to my mind when I think of Brook Berringer is what became his focus in the last year of his life. He was living for something far beyond the temporary, extending into eternal life. I saw in him a desire to experience Jesus Christ and to know His power, living it out in his daily life.

It's incredible how Brook's death shined light on his spiritual life. People from all walks of life already had a high opinion of him. It made profound sense and brought comfort to many that Brook received Christ and that through Christ his life was truly transformed.

During the fall of 1994, he burst into the national spotlight. In a run of eight games, after Tommie Frazier went down with a blood clot, he led the Big Red through the heart of the Big Eight schedule. He started seven of those games, finished the other, played with a deflated lung, was undefeated, and put our team in position to play for the national championship.

For eight months then, controversy boiled about who would be the starter in the fall of 1995. When Frazier was chosen, Brook became our backup quarterback.

The 1994 football season had proven to be a great success for Brook from the world's perspective. He was an outstanding quarterback and Nebraska surely wouldn't have won the national championship that year without his efforts.

However, even though he played sparingly, the 1995 season was his greatest. ESPN claimed at the time that the Cornhusker team that year was the most dominant ever. Though he often sat on the bench in obscurity, Brook was the most important influence on that team. Because of his devotion to the team–instead of fostering a quarterback controversy–he demonstrated the fruit of the Spirit working in his life. He could have divided the team on the issue, but he took the exact opposite attitude. Seldom do you see such a selfless attitude in sports or life in general. That bold humility became glaringly evident at his death. As a result, God used his death to bring many of his teammates to a saving knowledge of Jesus Christ.

Like God's plans for us, it wasn't immediately clear how He would use Brook's life. As details of his life became known, people began to take a long look, not only at his life, but also at their own.

What I remember most about Brook, what stands out to me, and what inspires me most, is that he was a player whose role became less his senior year, but his contribution became greater. Brook was a servant leader. It wasn't that he thought less of himself but he simply thought about himself less. Our Lord Jesus Christ put it this way, "But whoever would be great among you must be your servant" (Mark 10:43).

Ron Brown
Assistant Football Coach
University of Nebraska - Lincoln

INTRODUCTION BY JAN

It was a beautiful late spring snowfall. Mail wasn't being delivered that day because of the deep snow so I drove down to the post office in four-wheel drive to pick up my mail. I was expecting something very special and I wasn't disappointed.

It was a proof copy of Sawyer Brown's "The Nebraska Song," written about Brook and Tom Osborne by Mark Miller. Mark sent it to me so I wouldn't have to wait until the CD came out to hear it.

I drove out to the cemetery and listened to it by my husband's (Warren) and son's (Brook) headstone. The snow was swirling in my eyes while memories were swirling in my head as I listened to the song the second time. In my memory, I could hear the voices and laughter of my children as they enjoyed late springtime snowstorms in the past. In my minds eye, I was taken back to times like when the kids took the three-wheeler to the high school track just behind our backyard. Nicoel and Drue put on their plastic skis and Brook tied two water ski ropes behind the three-wheeler and pulled them around the track in the deep snow.

I remembered the time we had a snow drift that went up to the roof. They had fun climbing up to the roof and jumping down the drift. Freckles would bounce along trying to keep up with them in the snow.

I took pictures of them building a snowman with their daddy when they were little. Hot chocolate and cookies followed.

And I relived the day Brook left to go to Nebraska at seventeen years old to join the Big Red freight train.

When the song ended, all was very quiet. I blinked back the past and focused on my surroundings. I studied Warren's name, then Brook's name on the headstone. Two very special guys whose lives were cut much too short.

I looked around at other headstones. I noticed the dash–the names on all the headstones had a dash or a space between the date of birth and the date of death. I returned my focus back to that space between Warren's dates and Brook's dates. The realization of that little space and what it stands for was suddenly overwhelming. That dash, that tiny little dash, represented all the living that happened between those dates, the date when they were born and the date when they died.

I thought of when Warren and I started dating in high school. I was attracted to his kindness, thoughtfulness, integrity, family values, and his distinct sense of right and wrong, which of course was right after first noticing that he was really cute and a lot of fun.

I thought of stories and pictures of his childhood antics with his twin brother.

I thought about how proud he was of each of his children and how he was so determined to help each of them reach their potential and to always know how much he loved them.

I thought of the dash between Brook's dates. He was a very busy and fun little boy. I reflected on some of the memorable times that he, like all little kids, said or did some very funny things. One of my favorites was when he was about four and wanted to make chocolate chip cookies. I got everything out and Brook pushed a chair over to the counter top to stand on so he could help. When I opened the refrigerator, I remembered that we were out of eggs. I asked Brook if he wanted to call Grandma and see if we could get a couple of eggs from her. My parents lived just a block "as the crow flies" from us. So Brook climbed up on the cabinet and sat crossed legged in front of the phone. He dialed and then I heard his side of the conversation: "Hi Grandma, this is Brook. Grandma, do you have.....(pause)..... Brook..... (pause)..... Grandma, do you have 2 eggs? Brook.....(pause)..... Grandma, we're making chocolate chip cookies. Do you have.....(pause)..... Brook Berringer." After a short pause, he laughed and shouted, "YEAH, AND I'M SUPERMAN!" He held the phone away and said, "Hey, mom, Grandma's acting like she's Mrs. Jones!" I stopped and then as it dawned on me, I grabbed the phone and said, "Hello?" Mrs. Jones said, "Someone thinks he's talking to his grandma, but this is Neva Jones." I apologized for the misdial and we called my mom.

On his sixth birthday, we had a birthday party at our house. Mom came over for the party and enjoyed all his little friends. She watched as he opened all his gifts, including the one from her, which was a pair of green jeans that were not only out of style but also about two sizes too big, the kind you'd find on the sidewalk sale.

After the party, mom told Brook that he had such a nice birthday with such nice friends. As she was looking at his pile of toys he opened, she said, "Wow, you got so many nice presents. Tell me, what is your favorite present?" This was so out of character for my mom to ask such a question, but she smiled about his answer for years. He looked at her with a questioning look, considered his answer for a few moments, then said, "Uhmm......., what was that you gave me again, Grandma?" It was going to be his favorite thing if he could just remember what it was. Always the diplomat.

The long time spent at the cemetery that day allowed me time to reflect on the incredible lives that this father and son spent on this earth. It was the beginning of my task of learning how to manage grief. Many times when I feel the edge of despair beginning to sneak in, I stop and reflect on the wonderful lives that Warren and Brook led. Even though much too short, they both packed a lot of mileage into their short dash.

Someone sent me the following verses:

I read of a man who stood to speak
At the funeral of a friend.
He referred to the date on her tombstone

From the beginning to the end.

He noted that first came her date of birth
And spoke the second date with tears.
But he said what mattered most of all
Was the dash between those years.

For that dash represents all the time
That she spent alive on earth
And now only those who loved her
Know what that little line is worth.

For it matters not how much we own,
The cars....the house....the cash.
What matters most is how we live and love
And how we spend our dash.

So think about this long and hard...
Are there things you'd like to change?
For you never know how much time is left
That can still be rearranged.

If we could just slow down enough
To consider what's true and real,
And always try to understand
How other people feel.

And be less quick to anger,
And show appreciation more
And love the people in our lives
Like we've never loved before.

If we treat each other with respect,
And more often wear a smile...
Remembering that this special dash
Might only last a little while.

So, when your eulogy's being read
With your life's actions to rehash,
Would you be proud of the things they say
About how you spent your dash?

Author Unknown

I'm so thankful for the continued outpouring of love and support that my family has received during the past 15 years. It's humbling to see how many friends and football fans were impacted by my son's brief life. I trust you will enjoy the reflections from the past 15 years since my son's death and its impact through this book and his life. I'm especially pleased that his legacy is remembered through the Brook Berringer Citizenship Team which is awarded to deserving football players each year. We have placed a list of the award winners since 1997 in the back of the book.

Wishing you God's richest blessings.
Jan Berringer

PROLOGUE

I t is unusual that the beginning of a biography should look first to the ending, but you will find that this is a most unusual story. On April 21, 1996, I had the privilege of speaking at the funeral service for Brook Berringer in Goodland, Kansas. I began by stating that he was "the finest man I've ever known."

My statement was not merely an emotional response to the grief I felt. It was something I had believed for many months. There was never any doubt that Brook was someone with great moral character. In the process of becoming friends with Brook, I learned that his parents had taught him well. Both his mother and father were powerful figures in his life even though he was only seven years old when his father died. His mother kept Warren's memory alive in Brook and his sisters. She told them on more than one occasion that she and Warren had agreed on the way they were to be reared. By her firm moral hand on his life, his mother became the most important person in the world to him.

Those two forceful influences contributed to what became in Brook a powerful capacity to accept whatever came into his life–good or bad, and process it into a positive strength for himself and a blessing to others.

In a sense, I became Brook's spiritual mentor the last year of his life. We talked and prayed together regularly. I had the privilege of encouraging and challenging him in his walk with God. But there are many other people–relatives, friends and loved ones–who were just as close if not closer to Brook than I was. So I do consider it an honor to share with you from my vantage point what made this young man special. A man who received adulation from old and young alike wherever he went, not because of any particular accomplishment, but because of who people sensed he was . . . someone unique. And they were right.

On the night of April 18, 1996, being interviewed by Ken Hambleton, sportswriter for the *Lincoln Journal-Star*, I asked him, "You know the clean-cut Brook Berringer you've talked to and known and seen and written about for years?"

"Yes," he responded.

"He is exactly the same on the inside," I stated.

While Brook was never to be drafted by the National Football League, due to his untimely death, in a very real sense he was chosen in a heavenly draft. And while we'll never know how high he would have been picked in the NFL, I can assure you, from my perspective he was one of God's No. 1 draft picks!

At the end of a long telephone conversation with his mother the night a plane crash took his life on April 18, 1996, I told Jan, "Brook was too good for this world."

In the days since then, I have realized that one reason for my own grief and anguish was that the universe was thrown out of balance temporarily. Heaven gained a treasure it deserved while earth lost a man it did not deserve.

Perhaps telling his story, from my perspective, will return a bit of balance to an otherwise awkward world.

Who then was Brook Berringer?

I can hardly wait for you to see.

CHAPTER 1

FATHER/SON

E veryone who knew Brook Berringer well, certainly understood one thing about him: his dad, Warren, was the most important influence in his life, his primary role model. The significance of that relationship flavored every aspect of Brook's life.

In discussing the eventual writing of this book just four weeks before he died, Brook and I agreed that the first chapter would be about the relationship he had with his dad. His father's love, more than any other bond, determined the course of his son's life.

Brook's earliest remembrances of life were not of nursery rhymes or children's books or toys, but of walking out in broad fields and along quiet streams with a tall, lean man who loved and adored him.

The heart of the father/son bond was not partial or one-sided. It was full and complete with two equal participants. Though certainly Warren was the mature contributor to the relationship, they were equal learners. Brook's intense interest in knowing everything about everything pushed his father continually to keep pace.

When Brook was born in Scottsbluff, Nebraska, on July 9, 1973, Warren's first, loving view of him was a tiny figure with lots of black hair, cradled in his mother's arms. Tears of joy welled up in his eyes. "He's beautiful," he said simply to Jan as he leaned over to kiss her. Then, tenderly, he lifted his son into his arms and walked quietly around the room, voicelessly expressing his thanks to God. He knew that this little life, entrusted to him and his wife, just as daughter Nicoel before him, was a gift from above.

Warren had been excitedly awaiting his son's arrival. Four years prior, Warren and Jan attended a University of Nebraska football game with their good friends Jerry and Jeanne McCue. Later that night, Warren told Jan, "Wouldn't it be something if we had a son who played for the Cornhuskers someday?" Warren had discussed at great length with Jan the things he was going to teach and do with his son. The day Brook was born, Warren bought his boy his first baseball glove.

Before Warren brought Jan and Brook home from the hospital, he also sought to purchase Brook's first fishing license. He went to Tempo which, among other things, sold hunting and fishing supplies.

"I want a fishing license for my son," Warren proudly stated.

"Okay. What's his name?" the clerk asked.

"Brook Warren Berringer."

After asking Brook's address, the clerk then asked his date of birth to which Warren replied, "July 9th, 1973."

"No," the clerk said, "I don't mean when he had his birthday this year. I need to know his birth date."

"July 9th, 1973."

"You don't get it, do you?" the clerk said as he was starting to get annoyed. "I need to know when your son was born."

"July 9th, 1973," replied Warren rather triumphantly.

The clerk looked at him and said, "You have to pay for this, you know."

"I fully intend to."

"Height?"

"Twenty-two inches . . ."

Warren went directly back to the hospital and placed his son's first fishing license in front of Jan and said, "Well, I got that taken care of."

Brook grew to be as proud as his dad was of this license. It hung on his bedroom wall at home until he took it with him to college.

A few weeks later, when Jan's sister Jo and her husband, Stan, came to visit, Warren proudly held up Brook for the motion picture camera as if he were displaying a trophy. Even at that early age, it could be seen that the boy had inherited traits from both sides of the family—height from the Berringers, broad build and muscle from the Ochsners. Two additional family characteristics developed in the child, and were clearly discernible later in the young man: the work ethic from his mother's side, and the great love of the outdoors from his father's side.

The idol of his life was his dad. Sure, he loved his mother who took care of the cuts and bruises, and cooked the fish and wild game. But it was with his dad that he had the adventure of getting the cuts and bruises, and catching the fish and watching the wild game fall. Before Brook could hold a pole over the water or lift a shotgun to his shoulder, Jan would pack a lunch bag and diaper bag for their hunting and fishing trips.

One such hunting trip proved to be of lasting significance. Warren's truck broke down and he lifted the hood to work on the engine. Anxious to get it fixed, and working in the cold temperature, he wasn't as careful as usual and the screwdriver he was using slipped and jabbed him in the eye. He winced in pain for a couple of minutes, finished the repair, and returned home later that day with his usual hunting limit. A short time later infection set in, which eventually required a cornea transplant. Due to the high dosage of anti-rejection drugs prescribed to treat his injury, his immune system was weakened and he later contracted cancer.

Even with that difficulty, Warren never lost his zest for life.

Warren was unable to work during much of this period due to the surgeries and hospital stays. As a result, he lost his position as the manager of a hotel in Scottsbluff. An innkeeper needs to be available 7 days a week, 24 hours a day. There was no time for tragedies.

Warren and Jan decided to return home to Goodland, Kansas, to "start over." The family moved in to live with her parents for a one year period. It was a difficult decision but they knew they needed help–and were thankful that family was there to provide that help. Warren found work at the feed lot initially and soon after put his business degree to use by serving as the manager of the Goodland Chamber of Commerce. Jan began working as an elementary school teacher.

This period proved to be an important bonding time for Brook with his Grandpa Ochsner. He saw firsthand in those formative years, and heard the stories repeated many times later, of the man's incredible tolerance for pain.

Once, his grandfather broke a big toe after dropping a piece of heavy farm equipment on his foot. Then, he simply splinted it himself with a popsicle stick.

With a fiftieth wedding anniversary of his sister Matilda on the horizon, his daughter Jan challenged him, "Everyone else is going to be up in Sutton, Nebraska, having a great time and you're going to be sitting around with your foot propped up."

His wife, Ann, demanded that he go to the doctor, saying, "We need to X-ray it to see if it's broken."

"I know it's broke!" Edmund Ochsner replied.

Finally, he removed the homemade splint and went to see the doctor. After the X-ray, the doctor told Edmund to go home, splint his toe with a popsicle stick, and presented him with a bill.

Grandpa Ochsner was furious with his family, "Wasted $30!" he declared.

Such strength against pain was an important building block in young Brook's life.

Warren knew that his time on earth was limited. He'd had great years of romance with Jan. Their bond of love was strong and unbreakable. His only regret was that he wouldn't be around to see his three children grow and mature. (Brook's sister Drue had come along by then.) Therefore, he didn't give a second thought to taking Brook out of kindergarten for a four-day antelope hunting trip to Wyoming. The vivid details of that trip etched themselves into the heart and mind of the five-year-old as a joy that would last forever. He loved trudging through the knee-deep snow. And though he had to take two steps to his dad's one, he was determined not to embarrass his dad by falling behind the other men.

When the first day's hunt was ended, his heart raced with excitement as they returned to camp to cook over an open fire. He sat on a log and listened to the teasing his dad endured for not having gotten a shot off all day. His dad didn't respond with words; he intended to answer with action. As Brook snuggled in the warmth of his sleeping bag, lying next to his father in the tent, he was glad that his dad hadn't felt it necessary to defend himself. He knew his dad would prove himself. He was so proud of his dad. He wanted someday to be just like him.

They had seen a lot of game, but it wasn't until the third day that Warren got a clean shot at an antelope. With one expert squeeze of the trigger, the beautiful animal fell dead to the ground. Brook looked in awe as his dad stood reverently over his prize. In that moment, as Brook rubbed his fingers along the awesome antlers, he felt a special admiration for his dad, a unity in spirit. It was an exhilaration he'd never forget—there with the hero of his life.

In the two years following that trip, Brook didn't really grasp the significance of the fact that his dad's twin brother, William, came to visit more and more frequently. The two brothers were close friends and William wanted to be with Warren as much as possible to encourage him in his suffering from the spreading cancer. "But it worked just the opposite," William said. "As I watched Warren endure the pain quietly and without complaint because of his faith in God, my own faith was strengthened. I became a firm believer in Christ because of the testimony of his life."

Brook watched, warily. His dad continued to make trips to Colorado Springs and MD Anderson Hospital in Houston for treatments. Brook didn't understand the awesome significance of life and death, nor exactly what cancer was. But he knew what it meant to be hurt and how to cry. Most every night for the last two years of Warren's life, Brook would bring his sleeping bag to his father's bedside to fall asleep while holding Warren's hand. He could see that his beloved father was hurt, yet the man didn't cry or complain. Instead, his dad used all the more of his energies to bring joy to the lives of others. Brook was very young in years, but he saw and understood what a great impact his dad's positive attitude had on those around him. As a child, all he wanted was to be like his dad.

Warren was in and out of the hospital several times during those difficult years, but never once did he fail to lift others up by the grace he exhibited. He and Jan talked passionately of their combined hopes for the children. He knew that the task of rearing the three of them was going to be difficult and he encouraged her to be strong. She was determined in spirit that it would continue to be a joint effort.

Warren's pain was now getting to be unbearable. He could barely crawl, let alone walk across the living room floor. The doctors were persistent in their advice that Warren check in once again at the hospital so he could be given a steady supply of medication. He was resistant, however. There was one thing he wanted to see before surrendering to the cancer. He wanted to see Brook bag his first pheasant. Anyone who is a stranger to the sport might not understand such a determined desire. And those who are familiar with pheasant hunting might think it an impossible desire to fulfill. After all, how much could one expect of a kid who was only seven-and-a-half years of age? The shotgun was nearly as tall as Brook was!

Warren knew his son; and he was confident that Brook could shoot his first pheasant.

In hunting any bird, there are several things which must happen sequentially. Each step always requires split second timing. Once a bird dog has come to a point, the hunter must be ready to lift his weapon, figure the flight of the bird, lead it with his shot, and pull off the round–a lot to expect of a little kid. But Warren knew his son could do it. Brook did, too.

They headed into the country in grandpa's pickup truck with their Brittany Spaniel hunting dog, Freckles, who always sat up front. Brook had seen his dad bag his limit of pheasants many times before, but this was to be his day alone. His dad didn't carry a gun. Patiently they walked through the tall grass together. In a matter of minutes the dog stopped. "There's a point, son," Warren said loudly so the dog could hear as well. The next minute blurred into eternity as the pheasant took wing and Brook took a shot . . . and the bird kept on flying.

"You have to lead him," Warren advised quietly.

"Yeah, I know," Brook responded glumly.

"Don't worry," his dad cheered him on. "He'll scare up another point in a minute. Just be ready."

Brook missed a second and a third time.

On the fourth point, he was determined not to disappoint his dad again. He had been so anxious the first three times that he only used one shot. "If you miss the first time," he thought to himself, "try again." When the pheasant lifted in flight, Brook fired and missed, but he led the bird and fired again.

Brook would never forget what came next. A puff of colorful feathers flew up through the air as the pheasant slid in an arc toward the ground.

"You got him!" His father exulted.

That was a cheer which was more meaningful to him than any he would ever hear.

Whip-stepping through the tall grass he rushed forward to where the dog had retrieved the bird, holding it loosely in his jaws. Just as he'd seen his father do many times before, he took hold of the bird and tugged while saying gently, quietly to the dog, "Okay, I've got him. I've got him."

Reluctantly, yet obediently, Freckles let loose of the prize.

"Good dog! That's a good dog," Brook bragged as he rubbed his companion on the head.

In coming years, Brook would become an expert marksman and hunt all kinds of game in countless fields all over the plains; but the treasure of that moment would be the hunting thrill of his life.

A week later his dad, unable to ignore the excruciating pain any longer, checked into the hospital. On April 15, 1981, Warren Berringer, full of faith in God, was emptied of this life and ushered into eternity. His funeral took place on Good Friday, April 17, 1981.

It was a deeply traumatic time for the boy, not yet eight. He looked at the body of the man he adored, lying still in the polished wood coffin. Brook had barely begun to understand life. He certainly didn't understand death. He looked up at his mother, standing beside him. He knew she loved his dad as much as he did; and yet there was a calmness about her, a serenity of acceptance he couldn't understand. He put his arm around her as tears slid down his cheeks. He knew his mother was in great pain, yet she was giving such comfort to him, and to others. Brook wanted to be just like his mom.

CHAPTER 2

TIME TO SWIM

"A tragedy in your life–a time of great sorrow like that–is life changing. It's either going to make you or break you. You'll never be the same," said Jan Berringer. "You're going to either be better or worse. And I was determined we were going to be better for it. We weren't going to be the same. We couldn't be without Warren here. So we were going to make the most of it and benefit from it in anyway we could. We were going to be more compassionate and understanding of people who go through things like this. We were going to go on, we were going to have strength and courage and we were going to be a strong family even without Warren."

For Jan Berringer, it was either sink or swim. Lost were the hopes and dreams she and Warren had shared about building a strong and proud family together. Lost was the partner with whom she had planned on growing old. But Jan knew, too, that harboring bitterness, sorrow and any feeling of being cheated in this life would be destructive to the foundation she and Warren had already established in each of their children.

For Jan, it was time to swim.

Her first challenge was to understand how her role in her children's lives was going to change. For Brook, cooking meals, washing clothes and tenderly caring for his bumps and bruises would no longer be enough. She had to provide him with guidance, encouragement, and the role models he needed for an accurate perspective of what it meant to be a young man.

Jan heard what well-meaning friends said to her son at the funeral of his father, that he had now become the "man of the house." It was a cliché sort of thing to say, but not very wise. That wasn't what she needed. She didn't want him to become a man overnight–an absurd impossibility anyway. She and Warren had discussed this very thing. It would be difficult without her husband, but she wanted Brook to be a little boy. After all, he was just finishing the second grade.

Nonetheless, Brook took the suggestion seriously. He now had big responsibilities. Yet there was a pain in his heart that wouldn't go away. He had to deal with it. That night, long after the house had grown quiet, Brook lay awake, longing to be with his father. He tried to imagine what heaven was like. He didn't know. Was his father happy there? He drew a blank.

"Are you okay, Dad?" he asked.

But now there was no answer.

He had asked the same question the last time he saw his father at the hospital. He shuddered momentarily as he thought of that sick room with all of its tubes and machines which he hated. His dad's response then was weak, but precise, "Yes, Son, I'm fine."

Brook wanted to hear those words of reassurance again. However, he was surrounded by only stillness. "Heaven must be a long way away," he reasoned.

His eyes moistened as sadness engulfed him. He really missed his dad. He was about to sink into sorrow and self-pity when an inner strength suddenly emerged to lift him.

"Dad didn't cry," he whispered to himself, remembering the man he loved. "He fought the pain and didn't give in.

"I will too. I'm going to be like Dad."

With the determination of that goal, he sensed a oneness with his father and knew his dad was proud of the way he handled the pain. He rolled over and went to sleep.

The months to follow brought many challenges and changes to the Berringer household, and Jan watched with mild concern as Brook became more determined each day to become "the man of the house." He knew to be like Warren Berringer was a tall order. His dad towered 6-foot-2, knew everything about everything, and was wise and kind and understanding. But he'd be like that, too. At least he'd do his best.

He began by assuming a protective attitude toward the three women in his life. His dad would never let anything bad happen to any of them, so to Brook this was a necessary starting point of his responsibility.

Not long after his father's death, the family arrived home one night to find that a strong wind had blown the front door open. Remembering what his father had done in a similar situation, Brook hopped out of the car and ran to the house to make sure everything was safe.

With as much of a Warren tone to his voice as he could muster, he said, "Let me check things out first," as he examined the scene. While Jan carried things from the car to the house, she was heartbroken at the thought of her little boy feeling like he needed to be anything more than that. She certainly didn't want to do anything to crush his spirit, but she also wanted him to be free to enjoy all the exploring adventures a child of eight should have without the burden of being "the man of the house." His sisters, on the other hand, watched with admiration as their brother courageously inspected the house, and after a few minutes, gave his stamp of approval for their entrance.

From the earliest experiences with his sisters, Brook had an unbreakable code of honor toward them—no matter what they did to him—he never tattled on them to his parents. Nor did he hold their misdeeds over their heads. They learned that they never had to fear retribution from him.

Nonetheless, he also had a high standard for them which sometimes ran contrary to their desires. One day, while in high school, Drue came home furious with her brother after hearing that Brook had told one of his best friends that he wouldn't allow him to take Drue to the upcoming school dance.

"You just can't go out with him," Brook declared.

"Why not?" Drue asked.

"Just because," her brother answered.

Drue insisted, "Well, I'm going."

"It'll be over my dead body!" Brook said with authority.

Before tempers could get out of hand, Jan intervened and asked, "What's going on?"

Brook stated the problem in very simple terms.

No one spoke for a moment.

"Boy! I can't wait until he graduates!" Drue declared as she left the room.

Brook and his mother smiled knowingly at one another.

For Brook, such moments were a catharsis as the pain of missing his father was intense. Jan continued to search for ways to fill those voids that Warren's passing had left, but nothing could replace the pleasure of tossing a ball or walking the fields with him. However, Brook did find that every time he did something for someone else he could almost feel his dad's presence, almost a hand of approval on his shoulder. In a unique way, he practiced as a child what most people fail to learn in a lifetime. That the only lasting satisfaction in life is gained by giving—giving not so much of what you have, but of who you are.

In that respect, the lanky kid stored up another invaluable lesson in his heart. Even in a small town like Goodland, Kansas, there were lots of heroes. From his point of view, they were generally basketball or football players. On several occasions Brook would have given his right arm to have had the nerve to walk up to one of them to ask for an autograph, but he was too shy. He decided that if he ever had the chance to be celebrated, he'd watch out for the little kids standing at the back of the crowd. He'd make sure that anyone approaching him would know that for that moment they were the most important person in his life. He knew the anguish of wanting to reach out to someone great, only to have the desire squashed by timidity.

His mother, meanwhile, working as an elementary school teacher and sometimes an additional two other jobs, did make certain that her son had every opportunity feasible to pursue his obvious, natural talents in athletics. Like his father before him, he concentrated on basketball and football (though he also loved pitching in little league baseball). Warren and his twin brother, William, had been members of legendary sports teams at Goodland High. Their football team was undefeated their senior year, and their 1959 basketball team also won the state championship. (When that team was later inducted into the Kansas Basketball Hall of Fame in Topeka, Kansas, in 1993, Brook accepted the award on his dad's behalf.) William went on to become a scholarship quarterback at Colorado State. Warren decided to walk on at CSU to play halfback. But after taking 21 credit hours his first quarter at his advisor's suggestion, along with working 20 hours a week at a filling station to pay bills. Warren decided something had to give. He stopped taking classes his sophomore year in order to concentrate on earning money to pay for school. The Vietnam era had begun and soon after Warren returned home, he received his draft notice. Warren called his future wife at Colorado State College (now the University of Northern Colorado) and told her the disappointing news. Both of them were distressed with all of the uncertainties that go along with being personally involved in a war. He decided since he had to go, he'd prefer to serve in the Air Force.

Soon after Jan graduated with a teaching degree, she and Warren were married and shortly after that, Warren received orders to be stationed in the Philippines for 18 months. So only three months into their marriage, Warren was sent overseas . . . with his new bride soon to follow.

In Brook's critical, maturing years of pre-adolescence, with the steady encouragement of his mother, there wasn't anything within reason—sometimes even beyond—that he wasn't willing to try. He yearned to experience, to push the limits, of all the fantastic avenues of life. His interests were endless. However, his natural inclinations, and his concerted efforts were in those things where his father had influenced him—hunting, fishing—and sports of all kinds.

When Brook was eight, Uncle Willie invited Jan's family out to Colorado during spring break to teach them how to snow ski with his family at Ski Eldora. After getting the equipment rented, the tickets purchased and Nicoel's boot problems taken care of, both families huddled together for the day's instructions. Suddenly, someone noticed that Brook was missing. As they looked for him, they spotted him going up a T-bar lift.

Uncle Willie yelled, "Hey, Brook, have fun getting off!" Since Brook was only eight years old and inexperienced, Uncle Willie predicted, "He's going to wipe out when he gets off that thing," And sure enough, as soon as Brook hit the top of the hill, down he fell with skis and poles going in every direction.

As he worked at getting back on his feet, the families watched with interest as Brook considered his route back down the slope. Slowly, but with perseverance, Brook turned his skis around and began moving downhill. With each turn, he gained confidence and after several minutes reached the bottom of the hill, close to where his family was still waiting.

"Way to go, Brook," his mom yelled, delighted with her son's performance. Brook had made the first ski run of his life without falling even once. In fact, he skied the rest of the day without falling, an early indication of the God-given athletic abilities Brook was able to enjoy throughout his life.

Throughout his growing up years, Brook also thought and wondered a lot about God. He knew that was important to his dad, and his mother also encouraged him to be involved in church. He went to the youth group meetings at church, but there were so many other wonders of life begging for his attention. Brook knew he'd get around to it someday, but for the moment religion wasn't that important to him or many of his teenage friends.

Though they were the most important people in his life, Brook was fortunate that his mother and two sisters were not the only family he had. Jan saw to it that his extended family, the Ochsners and the Berringers, were all very much an integral part of his life. She knew that the love and support only family can give would be important for the children, and she was committed to spending as much time with them as possible. She had assured all three of her children that if ever there was a problem they didn't want to discuss with her, they had her permission to call long distance to their Uncle Stan in Indianapolis and talk it over with him. It was because of the wide range of ages of grandparents and uncles and aunts and cousins that Brook never experienced a generation gap. He was at total ease in relationships with old and young alike–even beyond the family.

Nonetheless, Jan was occasionally reminded that even with the family's love and support, she could not replace Warren. Once, after Brook had gone for what seemed like weeks without the opportunity to hunt, she offered to take him out to look for pheasants. As they climbed into their old Buick, the laundry list of things Jan still needed to do at home during her only day off began to roll through her mind. With dust pouring in from under the floorboards, Jan and Brook travelled down the back roads, searching for pheasants.

"You look over there, Mom, and I'll look on this side," Brook ordered. As they searched up and down the country roads, Jan soon began to realize that their seemingly hopeless journey couldn't be what Brook had in mind.

"Slow down, Mom! You're driving too fast," Brook demanded. Sadly, Jan turned toward her son and as he faced his mother, she said, "You know, Brook, I can't take Dad's place. There are some things I just can't do. I'll give you as many people to help as I can, but I can't do everything. You know I'd give anything to have your dad here to take you hunting, and I know you'd give anything, too. But that just can't be. I'm sorry."

As Brook sank into his seat, Jan tried to help soothe the painful reality that he would never again experience hunting as he had known it with his father.

"Brook, if I let you drive to the highway, could we go now?" Jan asked.

"Sure, Mom," Brook replied. So the two switched places, Jan put her leg on the seat to help prop Brook up over the steering wheel, and they headed for home.

Without his No. 1 hunting partner–his father–Brook never felt completely at home when he hunted with others. Often times, he felt like a fifth wheel when included on group hunting trips–the father/son relationship was painfully missing. But especially hurtful to his young spirit was not to be invited at all. On more than one occasion, when he knew others were going hunting, he sat ready and waiting by the telephone for hours. But it didn't ring.

Many nights his mother sat on the edge of his bed, rubbing his back, trying to console him as he cried out his pain. He found it difficult to put into words exactly what he was feeling, but he knew that when he was older he would never shut out anyone. That just wasn't right!

After Brook matured a few years, his father's twin, William, became more involved in his life. William, a commercial pilot for Delta Airlines, lived out-of-state and had a family of his own to care for, but he tried as often as he could to encourage Brook in his endeavors. His son, Todd, though six years older, also grew especially close to Brook after he arrived in Lincoln.

As time passed, it was only natural that Brook had an early attraction to flying. In fact, one of his early goals in life was to be a commercial pilot. To that end, he took his first flying lessons at the nearby airport. And later, his cousin Todd became Brook's flight instructor in Lincoln. His goal, just as in everything he did, was high. He wanted to pilot a jet. "Someday I'd love to fly with the Blue Angels," he envisioned.

Though, over a period of years, William and other relatives and friends became significant positive influences in Brook's life, they never replaced his father. Brook thought about and missed his dad every day. And he continued to take seriously his role as man of the house.

CHAPTER 3

REFOCUS ON FOOTBALL

About two weeks before Brook was to begin seventh grade, Jan drove her son to school to check out his football gear. Jan was going to wait in the car while he picked up his uniform. Brook put his hand on the door handle to get out of the car but stopped short, looked at his mom and asked, "Mom, if I ever get hurt out on the football field, are you going to come running out there?"

"You bet, Brook!" Jan asserted.

"Then I'm not going out for football," Brook replied as he took his hand off of the door handle.

"Wait a minute, Brook!" exclaimed Jan with a smile on her face. "Last year when Chris got hurt, his dad went running out there on the field for him."

"His *dad,* not his mom," said Brook.

"Oooh, mom's can't do that?" questioned Jan.

"No, and if you're going to do that then I'm not going out for football."

"What if you're bleeding to death out there?"

"Well, just say your goodbyes from your seat," Brook responded matter-of-factly.

"Okay," Jan promised, "if you ever get hurt on the football field, I'll never come running out there."

"Okay, Mom, you promised. Don't forget. And another thing, you never call the coach."

"Okay, I promise," replied Jan.

With that settled, Brook went into the school to check out his first set of football gear.

His first opportunities in organized football were less than impressive. It was obvious that he had natural athletic ability, but he had no one to help him one-on-one.

During that seventh grade season, Chris Wilson and Brook were vying for the coveted quarterback spot. Both of them were competitive kids and good athletes. Chris' dad and grandpa often came to practice and offered Chris valuable instructions and demonstrations. One night, Jan parked behind the Wilsons' pickup and waited for Brook to come out of the locker room. As Brook climbed into the car, he and Jan watched as Chris' mentors recapped the practice offering valuable words of encouragement and advice. Brook hung his head in sadness, and Jan vowed to herself to remember to park somewhere else next time.

That night, Jan heard Brook crying in his pillow. She sat down on the edge of his bed and tried to comfort him.

"I need my dad," Brook sobbed. "I need him to tell me what I'm doing wrong. I don't know what I'm doing. I'm doing something wrong and I'm not getting the football to go where I want it to go. Other kids' dads are telling them what to do."

Desperately concerned about Brook, Jan told her son, "Brook, I don't know anything about football, but I know somebody who does and I'll get you some help. Go to sleep and don't worry about a thing."

The next morning she called her friend Patty Thompson. Two of Patty and her husband Mac's three sons had been killed in an automobile accident not long after Warren's death. For the first three years after the accident, Mac couldn't bear to look at Brook because Brook reminded him of one of his sons that had been killed.

"Do you think Mac can be around Brook yet?" asked Jan. "Mac needs Brook and Brook needs Mac. Do you think he could talk to Brook about his football?"

Patty relayed the question to her husband and Mac immediately responded, "I can do better than that. I don't know anything about playing quarterback but I'll call my brother-in-law, Leo Hayden. He was quarterback at Goodland and at Fort Hays State. He can tell Brook what he's doing wrong."

That night when Jan and Brook got home from football practice, Leo was sitting in the driveway. She introduced Brook to Leo and they got started throwing the football to each other. As Jan watched them from the kitchen window, she realized that Leo had three kids and a wife who were probably waiting on him for supper; he had just got off work and was probably tired and hungry. Yet there he was out there running around the yard, working with her son.

Jan was elated that someone had cared enough to give her boy that little bit of added boost. She was doubly amazed when Leo showed up the next night–and the next–and the next. It was just the manly touch that Brook needed.

Later, when Brook's seventh grade team was scheduled to play a school team 30 miles away in St. Francis, the roads were an icy glare. Jan and Grandma and Grandpa Berringer made the trip. While sitting in the stands, Jan thought that no one in their right mind would be sitting there in those miserable, snowy conditions. However, in the progress of the game, she heard a voice behind her yell out, "Way to go, Brook!" She turned in amazement to see Leo Hayden cheering on his pupil. Leo was studying what Brook was doing so he could offer new suggestions the following week.

It was quite natural then that these two also became hunting and fishing friends.

As it is with most families, the Berringers, too, experienced the common ups and downs that come with the growing up process. Jan remembers Brook's freshman year as probably the most trying time on their relationship.

At one point, Brook had wanted to do something that most of his friends were going to do and Jan simply did not approve of the boys' plan. He pleaded and begged his mother to let him go, and she said "Brook, I've never given you strict rules and I don't tell you 'no' very often. So when I say 'no' I mean it." He was quiet for a moment, and then started pleading his case one final time.

"Brook," Jan continued, "When you were born your dad and I were so excited. We talked about how we would raise you and your sisters to be respectful and loving and generous to those around you. We agreed on everything, down to the last detail. Brook, your dad and I loved each other very much. He loved me as much as he loved you kids. And when I tell you 'no,' you're dad is telling you 'no,' too."

Brook looked into his mother's eyes and realized the hurt he had brought to her by arguing with her. His eyes welled up with tears and the two hugged for a long time. Brook understood that his mother truly had his best interest at heart.

During the summer following his freshman year, Brook set his eyes solely on the only position he wanted to play–quarterback. During his sophomore year he became the starting quarterback for the junior varsity team.

In basketball, on the other hand, even as a sophomore he was able to play some games for the varsity. The opportunity to be involved and his acceptance on the team spurred his interest in the sport. "I really liked basketball more than football," he said later, "and I thought I might be better college material in basketball."

Getting ready for his junior year, Brook was undecided on whether he should put his emphasis on the gridiron or the hard court. Unfortunately, he received some unwelcome help in making that decision. On just the third day of football practice, he was tackled hard. He got up limping, and the resulting injury developed into a deep thigh bruise. Missing the first five games all but eliminated his junior year season. He saw very little action and at the most took 30 snaps from behind center in the last few games of the year.

In basketball, however, he had an outstanding year and began drawing attention from several colleges. Brook averaged 11.5 points and 6.3 rebounds per game. He was selected to the Topside Tipoff All-Tournament Team and named to the All-Northwest League Team.

Brook was beginning to feel real pressure as his junior year came to a close. He knew that if he wanted a college education, family finances would be especially tight unless he landed a scholarship. There was no doubt about his talent as an athlete, nor did he take his physical blessing for granted. By then he had surpassed his Uncle Willie in height by stretching out to 6-foot-3. And, at 190 pounds, he was no longer lanky. His problem, however, was choosing between two sports he loved.

Conversations ensued with Brook's mother, cousin Tony Workman who had played college football, friend Dev Mull, high school coach Mike Johnson and Warren's former high school coach Duane Unruh. But, as always, Brook had to turn inward to determine his course. "I love basketball and enjoy it," he reasoned to himself. "But I have a real desire to prove myself as a quarterback. I think that's where I can excel."

The decision did not come easy, but with the endorsement of his mother and strong encouragement from Coach Johnson, he decided to go for it.

With fresh inspiration, Brook focused on what he needed to do. He knew that with just one more season of high school football to play, he'd have to use additional means to draw attention to himself from any prominent schools. Coach Johnson suggested he try to get into a couple of summer football camps. He applied to the Mile High Football Camp conducted by the Denver Broncos and was accepted. His other choice was the Big Red Football Camp at the University of Nebraska. Brook was late in applying for the Lincoln camp, which was at a 400-player capacity, but after Leo Hayden made a few phone calls, Brook was allowed to join the camp.

Two things of lasting significance happened when Brook went to Lincoln for the Big Red Camp. First and foremost, he loved the place from the start. He felt at home. Of equal importance, he caught the attention of the coaching staff after showing off his exceptional speed and a right arm that could rocket the ball downfield. More important than his passing skills (at a school where rushing the ball is still considered standard offense), was his exceptional effort in a touch football scrimmage. That instance even drew a bit of praise from Huskers Coach Tom Osborne. Brook dropped back to pass, but when he saw nobody open, he scrambled and weaved for 50 yards to a touchdown before anyone could lay a hand on him.

Osborne didn't say anything, but clapped his hands in appreciation and made some notes on his clipboard.

Brook was impressed with the attitude and thoroughness with which the coaches and staff approached their responsibilities. "I'd give my right arm to come here," he thought to himself. Immediately, he smiled when he realized his choice of words, "And that's just what it'll take."

While at the camp in Denver, Brook was enthusiastic about his decision to give football his best shot. He learned a lot brushing up against truly talented players from several states, and receiving instruction from some of the best coaches in the business. He truly loved the grueling toughness that was demanded of him. In turn, he pushed himself to excel. He came away with the thrill of having won the eye-hand coordination drill with Gary Kubiak, who at that point was the Broncos No. 2 quarterback. Kubiak assured him, "One day I'll be watching you play for the Broncos." Heady stuff for a kid from the plains of Kansas.

Basketball was now pushed way to the back of his mind. He refocused the rest of the summer before his senior year of high school, getting ready to be at his best for football. (Though, of course, fishing and water-skiing were not left to chance.)

In the fall of 1990, Brook had an outstanding passing and rushing season as the starting quarterback for the Goodland Cowboys. His effort earned him all-state honors in Kansas' third-largest school classification (4-A). Even at that, the 17-year-old senior was just coming into his own from a physical standpoint. He was a year younger than most of his counterparts. If he'd had another year to mature, he undoubtedly would have been a blue-chip prospect for almost any school in the country. Coach Johnson even quipped, "I wish I could've redshirted him a year."

Johnson observed, "Brook just graduated a year too early. Everybody in the country would have wanted him if he had been in high school a year longer. He was just a year away from tearing things up."

As it was, Ron Brown, the Cornhuskers receivers coach, was already on his trail with the recruiting assignment from Nebraska. Several schools were prepared to offer Brook athletic scholarships– Kansas, Kansas State, Fort Hays/Kansas State University, North Dakota and Wyoming. Washington State, Colorado State and Auburn also showed an interest in his talents. The University of North Dakota, a division II school, was very much in the running as they had an accredited flight training program. From there, Brook could graduate and go straight to piloting in the airlines.

Brook was excited about the flurry of attention coming his way, but there was only one school that had his interest. He really wanted Nebraska to want him. From the first time he walked into Memorial Stadium, he was sold on the outstanding facilities and the winning tradition. Along with solid academics, and what he'd heard of the fabulous fans, there was no other program, in his mind, that could compare with it.

He also had a deep admiration for Tom Osborne, and really connected in spirit with Ron Brown. He looked forward to Ron's visits to his home and Brook talked to Ron about how he had hunted whatever it was they were eating, even showing a framed picture on the wall with him on the wintry plains of Kansas with his prized kill of a coyote. Having grown up in the summer resort town of Martha's Vineyard, Ron knew nothing of trudging through knee-deep snow in zero weather to hunt.

Prior to his first visit, Ron talked to Jan about his trip west.

"I'd like to come out to visit Brook next week if that would be possible," Ron suggested.

"Sure," replied Jan. "When do you think you might be out?"

"How about Thursday evening around six o'clock?" Ron said.

"Okay. Have you ever tried pheasant?" Jan asked.

"No," Ron responded, "but I'm willing to give it a try,"

Pheasant fondue was Brook's favorite dish. In fact, Jan made an oversized batch this time, just so Brook would have leftovers to pop into the Fry Daddy when he was hungry throughout the week.

Leftovers, however, were not to be. The meal was a big hit, and

Brook, Ron, Jan, and Drue ended up consuming the entire batch of seven pheasants in that one sitting.

The next time Ron called to arrange a visit, Jan excitedly asked if he would be able to join them again for dinner.

"Has Brook been hunting lately?" Ron asked, remembering the fabulous fondue from the last meal.

"He shot three coyotes last week." Jan responded, "Are you game to try it?"

"Sure," Ron gulped. But he didn't ask any questions.

The next Thursday Ron arrived and he and Jan visited until Brook got home. When Brook came in from practice Ron rather quickly got to the meat of the matter, "Your mom said you've been hunting again."

Brook responded with pride, "Yep, I got three coyotes."

"Well, this will be a first for me," Ron said, hesitantly.

"What do you mean?" Brook asked.

"Eating coyote," Ron replied.

"Mom!" Brook chided his mother for her joke.

Ron smiled at being taken in by the ruse. "I guess no one really eats coyote," he said thankfully. They all laughed together, and bonded stronger than ever.

But Brook knew that Ron did know football–even if he didn't know the difference between a coyote and a prairie dog. In such give and take, the two built a relationship which was special to Brook.

Meanwhile, Brook was still a catalyst for Coach Don Smith's Goodland High School basketball team. Brook, along with senior starters Chris Wilson and Jason Hickson led their team to the State Championship Tournament. During the season, Brook averaged 17.4 points and 6.6 rebounds per game. He was again selected to the All-Northwest League Team and the Topside Tipoff All-Tournament Team. In addition, he was placed on the Colby Classic All-Tournament Team. Brook was chosen All-State Honorable Mention by the *Wichita Eagle-Beacon* and the *Topeka Daily Capital*. The *Salina Journal* selected him to their All-Area First Team Classes 4A-6A.

For months, Brook had been looking forward to his one official visit to the Nebraska campus allowed by the NCAA. His Uncle Willie accompanied him on the trip. Though he had his mother's unqualified support and it was already a foregone conclusion that Brook would play his college career at Nebraska, he was thankful for his uncle's reassuring presence. Brook stood tall and was an impressive figure, dressed in slacks, tie and his senior letter jacket as he walked in step with Tom Osborne to be introduced to the team.

There was one additional request he had, which most football recruits think nothing about. What sort of flying facilities were available for him? While the options for flying could have been better, Brook worked out flying opportunities to his satisfaction. His cousin Todd was his flight instructor and Brook was about to earn his pilot's license.

Nebraska had everything Brook wanted.

Most significantly there was a football program second to none in the nation. Though he had a strong passing arm and Osborne's strategy was built around a running game, Brook determined, "Whenever he calls for a pass, I want to be the man."

He hoped to have a chance to reshape the concept that most Cornhusker fans had of an option quarterback. Speaking of his high school experience, he said, "I dropped back and threw the ball but I also ran a lot of option. So I felt like Nebraska's offense would fit me well. I'm bigger than most people imagine an option quarterback to be. But I think I've got the speed to run the option and I've got the arm to throw the ball; and I think that's what they're looking for."

Beyond football, it was also of interest to Brook that Nebraska had wide open fields teeming with quail, pheasants, turkeys, ducks, and deer. There were lakes with game fish just waiting to be baited. His father before him had hunted across those prairies and fished those lakes, and that made it all the more special to him.

And, of course, he could still pursue his love of flying!

CHAPTER 4

THREE YEARS IN THE SHADOWS

Intending to get a head start on his college career, Brook wanted to go to Lincoln in June, 1991. There was a conditioning program and passing league (a practice time loosely organized by and for the players–no coaches allowed) in which Brook wanted to participate.

Brook packed his Mustang to the ceiling with his belongings and ran his errands before leaving town. He stopped to get gas and to say goodbye to both sets of grandparents, aunts and uncles, as well as Leo Hayden and his family. Brook then returned home to tell his mother goodbye. With tears streaming down both of their cheeks, Brook went to his mom, gave her a big bear hug and said, "I'm going to make you proud, Mom." As they hugged, Brook's nose began to bleed. (He always seemed to have a nose bleed at the wrong time.) Jan ran to get a washcloth. Her parting view of Brook leaving for his first year of college was him holding a cold washcloth to his nose and tears pouring down his cheeks as he walked down the driveway toward his car.

Since he had made his arrival intentions known to the Nebraska football staff, he assumed that when he got to Lincoln he'd have a job and a place to stay.

Wrong.

When he walked into the South Stadium offices for the first time that afternoon, he soon felt as though he were a stranger from outer space. It seemed to him, that nobody knew who he was, what he was to do, nor where he was to stay. "I'm on scholarship as a quarterback," he explained to a pleasant woman behind the desk.

"Oh, you're the one from Kansas," she realized at last.

Brook smiled with renewed hope.

"But everyone's gone for the day," she continued, "and I don't have any information. Can you come back after eight in the morning?"

"Yeah. Thanks," he said as he turned away to try to find the nearest telephone to call home. A sad sense of loneliness was his only companion.

"Mom," he greeted the familiar voice when she answered, "everything's messed up here. They don't have anything ready for me, not even a place to stay."

"Come home then, Brook. You've just gone up there too soon, " urged Jan.

Brook would have none of that. He was determined to make the situation work.

When he got back to his car, there was another surprise waiting for him on the windshield–his first parking citation. He held it in his hand for a minute, tempted to be upset at this further insult to his arrival. Then he chuckled out loud as he decided how to make maximum use of it. He tucked it back under the windshield wiper and walked around the building to check out things in the weight room before leaving campus.

Brook was unable to find room accommodations anywhere at first. Apartment costs were well over what he had budgeted to spend. He spent the first four nights in Lincoln sleeping in his packed car.

Later that same week in the Training Table area, he saw a familiar face. It was Lance Lewis, a member of the football team and a fellow Kansan.

"Listen," Lance said, "Coach Brown told me you had a lodging problem. You're sure welcome to stay with me tonight. I don't have an extra bed, but there's plenty of room on the floor."

"Great!" Brook agreed, heartened totally by the open invitation of acceptance. Always the optimist, he was anxious to greet the next day and get on with it. (Brook did find housing accommodations after his second night at Lance's apartment.)

Clester Johnson, from nearby Bellevue whom Brook had met and visited with at the previous spring game, had also been signed as a scholarship quarterback that year. After Clester saw him in action for the first time at the passing league, and observed his drop-back, pro-style passing, said to Brook, "You should be at Miami. What made you come here?"

"To beat you out of the job," Brook responded with a smile.

Clester looked at him quizzically, then laughed aloud. "You're all right, Berringer," he said without countering the challenge.

Tony Veland, from Omaha, was also in the big crop of 1991 scholarship quarterbacks (and probably the hottest prospect to get the job). He had a similar first impression of "the guy from Kansas," but he was also aware of Brook's reputation as a scrambler. "From day one I knew he was a good athlete," Tony said.

(In the course of their careers at Nebraska, Johnson developed into an excellent wingback and Veland became a defensive quarterback as a safety. And all three became good friends.)

But not everyone was ready to accept the new boy without putting him to the test. Because Brook was only 18 years old and was still a thin 190 pounds on a 6-foot-3 frame, he was not an over-powering figure. He was changing clothes in the locker room one afternoon after the veteran players returned for fall camp when he heard a few guys from behind making a variety of racial slurs. His first thought was one of disgust. He hated confrontation, but knew that he had to stand up for himself.

Finally, Brook mustered up the courage he needed, turned around and said, "I don't appreciate the comments you guys are making and I'd like you to stop." Just then, 10 other football players stepped behind Brook in his support and waited for the others' reaction. After a long moment, they turned away, mumbling to themselves. Brook's supporters went about their business with whispers of approval to each other. The new kid had passed the challenge.

From the beginning, Brook planned to redshirt his first year in Lincoln. He knew he had a lot to learn about football, having only played the one full season back in Goodland. Therefore, in that first fall as a Cornhusker, he quickly discovered that there were no easy lessons, and only a few bright spots. There were no immediate rewards in being a "tackling dummy" for the team. "It was tough," he admitted, "getting pounded on every day, knowing you're not going to play the whole season, and basically feeling like a nobody."

However, not being on the traveling squad did have its advantages. He was getting a decent start on his academic pursuit of a degree in Business Administration. Of almost equal importance to Brook though, was making contact with other hunters in the area and getting involved in Pheasants Forever, Quail Unlimited, and Ducks Unlimited. And, for added pleasure, having just qualified for his pilot's license, he was able to build hours in his log book.

That summer the Berringers and other extended family members decided to make the trek, as they had done so many times over the years, to Estes Park, Colorado. There was a spot not far from Estes that Aunt Jo and Uncle Stan had named "Warren's Meadow." It was a beautiful meadow between towering mountain peaks that Warren had "discovered" on one of the family's first trips to the area. It was one of his favorite places to take his family. To this day, the family feels close to Warren when they visit "Warren's Meadow."

While Brook and his Uncle Stan engulfed themselves in a conversation about Brook's first year of college, they took turns throwing rocks at a can about 30 yards away. Neither had experienced success in hitting it, however, and as Jan approached the two, she picked up a rock, threw it at the can, and hit it on her first attempt.

"Brook," Jan said, "when the reporters ask you where you got your arm, make sure you tell them you got it from your mother."

Brook and Stan burst into laughter, having been humiliated in their feeble attempts at knocking over that can.

With the previous season passing in a flash, Brook, having

grown another inch (6-foot-4) and gained 10 pounds (to 200), was back for the fall camp of what would be his first true year as a player. There were a dozen quarterbacks vying for the one position, with holdover Mike Grant ahead on the charts and Veland close on his heels. A highly touted new recruit from Florida named Tommie Frazier was also making his presence known. Brook was somewhere around fourth on the depth charts.

The home opener was against Utah and Brook was excited as he put on his uniform for the Big Red for the first time. He realized he probably wouldn't get into the game, but his emotions were running high. He'd heard from veteran players about the rush they got from pacing through the tunnel, then out into the stadium. And he was not disappointed. That first time he ran through the tunnel was a thrill he'd never forget. "When I ran onto the field," he said, "surrounded by my teammates, I had an incredible rush of emotion. The sea of red in the stands, the cheering fans, the total noise added up to an unbelievable experience."

Brook did get in the Utah game–for one series of downs. He was glad for that since members of his family had made the long trip to be there. But the remainder of the season began to take on considerable similarity to his redshirt year. He trained and practiced, but only played briefly in five games. He only threw the football twice. Therefore, it was difficult for him to feel like he was improving himself as a player. "I just wasn't getting the repetitions I needed," he explained. "It takes a while to grasp the offense and I knew I had to work on the little things to become a good player." He understood what the coaches expected of him, but without playing experience it was hard to improve.

Nonetheless, Brook refused to be discouraged. "I knew I was a very capable athlete," he said, "and all I wanted was a chance to develop and show my skills."

Meanwhile, Brook befriended a walk-on from nearby Wahoo, Nebraska–Matt Turman. Matt had played quarterback in high school under his father's coaching. Since he was only 5-foot-11, the Cornhuskers started him out as a receiver. Therefore, when he turned up for his first sessions of the passing league in 1992, he was on the other end of many of Brook's passes. Matt was later converted back to quarterback where he again earned the respect of the coaching staff. As they got acquainted, Brook and Matt became great friends and continually helped each other grow in their position at quarterback.

Brook enthusiastically looked forward to his sophomore season. He worked hard on the weights and added ten pounds of muscle, now up to 210 pounds. He performed well during the previous spring practice; and in the annual Red-White game completed 9 of 20 passes for 105 yards. Then in the first scrimmage of the fall camp, he hit 4 of 8 passes for 88 yards, including a 70-yard touchdown pass to tight end Trumane Bell. Brook was all set to play and greatly wanted to play. Quarterback Coach Turner Gill observed in August, "The public perception may be that he's forgotten around here. But people will be hearing about Brook Berringer–there's no question about it."

In the first game of the 1993 campaign against North Texas State, when the starter, Tommie Frazier, was sidelined with an ankle injury after only two plays, Brook got the first real opportunity of his college career and performed beautifully. On his first drive he connected on a touchdown pass to Corey Dixon. "I'll never forget that!" he declared. "I may connect on a thousand passes, but none will be sweeter than the first one." He went on to rush for two more touchdowns and wound up completing 7 of 7 passing attempts. With the game secure, and having advanced the ball to the 30-yard line, Brook was taken out to make way for Turman. Never in their relationship did he ever mind being replaced by Matt, "because," he said, "he deserves to play."

Turman, on the field for the first time as a player, was nervous beyond words at the thought of going into the game. Brook put his arm on his shoulder and gave him sound advice, which served to comfort him. "The first thing you want to do is get the snap," he told Turman. Matt heeded that simple advice, and after engineering a first down on the 15-yard line, he completed a pass for a touchdown on the first series of his college career.

Brook was then the first one on the field to tell him, "Good job," and give him a high five. The two shared a lot of football experiences together in the succeeding three years as roommates on all the team trips and the nights before the home games when the team stayed at the Nebraska Center.

Again in the Colorado State game, after Brook completed 4 of 8 passes (one for a touchdown), and had the Cornhuskers poised on the 15-yard line, Turman was given his second chance of the season. Instead of disappointment at not being able to complete the series into the end zone, Brook encouraged Matt, who then gained the first rushing touchdown of his career.

In the remainder of the season, Brook didn't see much more action. He mopped up against Missouri. Then when Frazier went to the sidelines twice in the second half of the Colorado game holding a dislocated shoulder in pain, Brook was called to the rescue. The same thing happened the following week on the road at Kansas. All told for the year, Brook rushed for two touchdowns and passed for two, completing 17 of 27 attempts for 222 yards.

Again Brook made the postseason trip to the Orange Bowl with the team, excited to be in what amounted to the national championship game. (The previous year he had watched the entire 60 minutes of the game as Nebraska lost.) Again he didn't get into the game, and again Nebraska lost to Florida State by the slim score of 18-16. "I wanted to be the guy out there doing it and not watching from the sidelines," he declared afterward. "I felt helpless and wanted in the worst way to become a more integral part of the team."

Even so, he remained optimistic. "You don't come here or anywhere else wanting to be the backup quarterback," he said. "I prepare as though I'm going to play every play."

The 1994 season didn't start all that auspiciously for Brook either. He was called on sparingly in the first three games against West Virginia, Texas Tech, and UCLA. Then he almost got his first start as a Cornhusker against Pacific. Coaches considered having Frazier sit out the game and rest a sore calf muscle which he had injured in the UCLA game.

The coaches decided to give Tommie the nod, hoping that his injury wasn't very serious. However, after taking just nine snaps, Frazier couldn't continue. Brook went in after a blocked punt by Barron Miles gave Nebraska the ball at the Pacific 19-yard line. On the first play he was sacked for a 5-yard loss. That, however, was about the only thing Brook did wrong the rest of the game. In the second quarter, he hit wingback Clester Johnson for a 15 yarder and tight end Eric Alford on a 46-yard play. He then finished Nebraska's first drive of the second half with an 18-yard touchdown pass to wingback Abdul Muhammad.

By the time he left the game in the third quarter, Brook had completed 8 of 15 passes for 120 yards. In seven series he guided the Cornhuskers to seven touchdowns. He scored on a 6-yard run and threw three touchdown passes during Nebraska's 70-21 rout. "It's important for me to get in and get some snaps and experience," he said after the game. "It helps with confidence. And as time goes by, the coaches feel more comfortable with my ability to run the offense."

Brook uttered those words not knowing that his days of obscurity were about to end. The next day Tommie was in the hospital because of a blood clot behind his right knee. He would miss at least the next game.

But not to worry.

Brook was declared the starter for the first time against Wyoming the following Saturday. He took the news in stride. "I prepare for every game like I'm going to start," he explained to the reporters who hovered around him on Monday afternoon. "It's no different for me."

CHAPTER 5

THRUST INTO THE LIMELIGHT

Prior to October 1, 1994, Brook Berringer was like the lonely Maytag repairman of the Nebraska Cornhuskers–everyone knew he was there, but no one needed his services. In three seasons he had had limited exposure in only 19 games and had watched the two previous Orange Bowl losses entirely from the bench.

When he first arrived in Lincoln, Brook admitted he had a lot to learn, having come from a relatively small high school. "I was pretty wide-eyed during my first couple of full-contact scrimmages. With as many quarterbacks as we had in my freshman year, I was a little bit intimidated." After redshirting that first year, he only played toward the end of five games during the 1992 season.

During his first two years in uniform, Brook was somewhat bothered by persistent bursitis in his right elbow. This problem was most likely caused by throwing too many curve balls in his younger years. With the help of medication and exercise, he was able to work through the pain and make his arm stronger than ever. Heaving the ball more than half a football field was no longer a problem.

Consequently, he entered his junior year in excellent health. Now that he had become familiar with the Nebraska offense, he was more confident in his ability to make the right decisions on the field. His timing on pass patterns was excellent and he ran out his fakes to perfection. Though his confidence level was high, he harbored doubts of getting any opportunity to see much action. There was no doubt that Tommie Frazier was the best option quarterback in college football. With Tommie's excellent work-ethic and commitment to improve his passing game, it was difficult for anyone to imagine Brook replacing him as the starter. Brook, however, continued on, undaunted by the level of competition facing him. He had worked hard and knew he could get the job done. "I want to show everybody what I can do when I get my chance," he declared.

The first three games of 1994 were in the pattern of the previous two seasons. He had seven yards rushing against West Virginia, one run for 15 yards in the Texas Tech game, and carried the ball twice against UCLA for 15 yards and one touchdown, and completed one pass for 12 yards. Then, in the fourth game against Pacific with Frazier injured, Brook saw more action than in all the other games combined. He carried the ball 6 times for 32 yards and a touchdown; and was 8 for 15 passing for 120 yards and 3 touchdowns. For the first time in his career at Nebraska, he entered the locker room after the game that afternoon with total enjoyment. Not only had the team won, but he had been called upon and had made a significant contribution to the victory. He had tasted the joy of success.

When Brook did get his opportunity, it was unexpected and not the way he wanted to get it. Frazier's injury was serious, even life threatening. He was sidelined by doctor's orders with blood clot problems. Brook was handed the ball to start against a strong Wyoming team. The chance he had yearned for and prepared for was suddenly upon him, and he seized it with a tenacity born of destiny. He connected on 15 of 22 passes for 131 yards and carried the ball 12 times for 64 yards and 3 touchdowns. On the first of those scores, just 12 seconds before the end of the first half, he was sandwiched powerfully by two Wyoming defenders. The helmet of the second man crashed into his side as he hit the ground. Brook had the luxury of lying there only a moment because, not knowing of his pain, teammates joyously jerked him to his feet.

During halftime, with his team down 21-14, Brook gave no thought to the ache in his side, rather concentrating on the task at hand. Sometimes struggling for breath, he played the second half with a partially-collapsed lung and cracked ribs. Clester Johnson later realized that Brook wasn't breathing right, so he asked him, "Why didn't you come out of the game if you knew you were hurt?"

With a gasp of breath Brook responded, "We had to win the game, man. I had to be in there."

Wyoming wouldn't have guessed he was injured by the way he performed at the start of the third quarter. He ran for touchdowns of 24 and 11 yards in the first seven minutes to cap a 28-point Nebraska burst in eight minutes.

Though the Cornhuskers were behind 14-0 early in the game, Brook held steady and proved his mettle in a tough situation. Except for a second quarter interception, his performance was practically flawless. After showering, he went to the interview room for his first notable meeting with a bevy of reporters. It was quite a shock for Brook to be the center of attention. The satisfaction in his expression was evident, but as always he accepted his success without any hint of pride. "After all," he explained in his matter-of-fact style, "it was a team effort."

He then returned to the training room because of chest pains, and after checking him over, the doctors sent him to Bryan Memorial Hospital in Lincoln. X-rays and tests revealed that his left lung was collapsed 40 percent. A small incision was cut in his left side to insert a tube to re-inflate the lung. He went home on Sunday and was back on the practice field on Tuesday, throwing the ball. "I thought I was just hurt," he said, "and had a bruise or something.

"There's a difference between being hurt and being injured. Everybody plays hurt sometime. It's hard to tell the difference because everybody plays through some pain."

To protect him against further injury, Brook was outfitted with a special flack jacket. "I feel like Robo-Cop," he joked as he trotted onto the field to start the next game against Oklahoma State. After hitting 10 of 15 passes for 75 yards in the first half, and with Nebraska ahead 9-3, X-rays taken during halftime showed that he had re-injured himself, and again his lung had partially collapsed. He sat out the second half while his buddy Matt Turman earned the title "Turmanator"–as the Cornhuskers finished out their sixth straight win of the season.

On the trip to Kansas State the following week, still nursing sore ribs, Brook did not start but watched as Turman led the offense through the first two quarters. However, holding only a 7-6 lead, Brook played the last series of the second quarter and started the second half. Without using Nebraska's standard pattern of options and quarterback keepers in order to protect his lungs from another direct hit, he marshaled the team to a 17-6 win against the highly touted Wildcats. (The outstanding play of the Blackshirts was the key to victory. They sacked NFL prospect Chad May 6 times for 53 yards in losses.)

In time for the Missouri game, Brook was back to nearly full throttle. After a slow start and no scoring in the first quarter, he directed a 14-play, 92-yard drive early in the second quarter to get the Huskers on the board. He went on to post his then-career-best 9 of 13 passing for 152 yards and 3 touchdowns, and rushed 5 times for 23 yards. Again the defense was stingy, giving up only a 34-yard touchdown strike midway through the fourth quarter. Nebraska waltzed away with a 42-7 win.

Colorado came to town the next week for a televised match-up of unbeaten powerhouses, No. 1 vs. No. 2. Brook was able to open up the offense, and proved his worth, leading the Huskers to a near perfect offensive execution against the Buffaloes. He connected on 12 of 17 passes for 142 yards, including a 30-yard touchdown toss that helped Nebraska gain a 24-0 lead. The Huskers' kicking game was a major contributing factor, as Colorado began 9 of its 13 possessions from its 20-yard line or worse. The 24-7 victory secured Nebraska in the No. 1 position in the Associated Press Poll.

The following week against Kansas, Brook completed 9 of 13 passes for 267 yards (the seventh best total in NU history), including two touchdown bombs. In the first half, he was 8 of 10 for 249 yards. He had a career-long 64-yard TD pass to one of his favorite targets, Clester Johnson, a 51-yard TD to Reggie Baul, and three other non-scoring passes over 25 yards. Nebraska won the game, 45-17.

The way Brook was playing, if Coach Osborne had wanted to run up the score and hadn't relieved him, he might have broken

David Humm's 1972 single-game Nebraska record of 297 passing yards. As it was, Brook called it, "A perfect day for football. The only thing I think it would be better for is quail hunting, and I'll take care of that tomorrow."

In advance of playing host to Nebraska the following week, Jim Walden, the Iowa State coach observed, "Berringer fits into the best offensive game plan in the country . . . he has added the dimension of throwing the ball, getting the big home run."

As if on cue, Brook proved him right. In his sixth start of the season, he was again over the 250-yard mark. He carried the ball nine times for 61 yards and hit 11 of 18 pass attempts for 193 yards. The passing yardage also put him over 1,000 for the season making him only the 19th quarterback in Cornhusker history to reach that level. His 460 passing yards against Kansas and Iowa State composed the best back-to-back passing games for a Nebraska quarterback since Vince Ferragamo in the 1976 season.

As always, Brook was quick to pass on the praise for his success to others. "You can give a lot of credit for the completion percentage to the amount of time and the protection I'm getting from the offensive line, and to the receivers for catching the ball.

"Sure, I got sacked twice, but the line can't hold a block forever. I take the blame for those sacks.

"When you've got as much time as I've got back there, you can pick guys apart."

The following week against Oklahoma, his seventh start, Brook had another good passing performance. After a slow start, he connected on 13 of 23 passes for 166 yards, and carried the ball 15 times for 48 yards. He scored the game's only touchdown in the third quarter from one yard out to cap a 10-play, 82-yard drive highlighted by a 44-yard pass to Abdul Muhammad on third-and-ten from the Huskers 43.

In recognition of his superb second half passing performance in the season finale against Oklahoma (completing 9 of 12 for 143 yards), he received the following letter:

December 14, 1994

Dear Brook:

On behalf of Chevrolet, congratulations on your outstanding performance on November 25, 1994 against University of Oklahoma. You can take pride in being selected as your team's "Most Valuable Player" by ABC Sports.

At the conclusion of the season, a special plaque honoring your accomplishment will be sent to your Sports Information Director for permanent display at your school. At the same time, you will receive a personalized MVP certificate plaque as a keepsake of your achievement. Also, in recognition of your team's appearance in that game, Chevrolet will donate $1,000 to your school's General Scholarship Fund.

Gary Gibbs, then Coach of the Oklahoma Sooners, touted Brook's performance. "He's extremely intelligent. If you watch him on tape, he has never put them in a bad play. I don't know how he grades out for them, but that's how I see it. Also, he's a better runner than people think. At 6-feet-4, he can jump up inside on an option and make something happen; and he has enough strength to see some extra yards when needed. And his passing is well-documented."

Certainly Gibbs was right about the passing. In completion percentage he led the Big Eight at .632, the best for a Nebraska quarterback in 20 years. Brook finished the regular season with a 7 and 0 mark as a starting quarterback. He had 1,295 yards passing and threw 10 touchdown passes. His pass efficiency rating was 149.9, which led the Big Eight, and would have ranked him seventh nationally if he had averaged 15 attempts per game. Over the final five games Brook passed for more than 100 yards each time and completed 65.2 percent of his passes (58-89 with two interceptions) for 920 yards (184 per game) and seven touchdowns. He started 99 drives and led NU to a score on 40 of them (35 TDs) for a 41.4 efficiency rating. He was 26-32 (.813) on drives in the red zone.

These statistics helped bring Brook out of obscurity to earn second-team All Big Eight honors. In response to that news, Brook said "I was a little bit surprised. But it's a neat honor, and I really do appreciate it."

When called to the task, he had proven himself worthy. Ignoring pain, which was his lifelong story, Brook carried on with the job handed to him. No one could have asked more. If they had, he'd have given it. He had marched the Cornhuskers through the rigors of a difficult schedule and left them poised on the pinnacle of the national college football scene, ranked No. 1.

The season had taken many strange twists and turns, with Brook particularly in the forefront. He wasn't concerned about being singled out for recognition and interviews. His desire was not so much to be recognized for what he could do, but to help his team win games.

In that respect, he was enthusiastic when asked about his responsibility in the only challenge that was left to a perfect 1994 season. With a confident smile, he replied, "Move the offense, get my job done. Nothing spectacular.

"Win the national championship."

That opportunity awaited in the Orange Bowl, January 1.

CHAPTER 6

QUARTERBACK CONTROVERSY

Brook's confidence level had never been higher than it was at the end of the 1994 regular season, which he had capped off with the lone touchdown in the Oklahoma victory. With the inconsistency of Nebraska's normally powerful running game against the Sooners (a season low of 136 rushing yards), Brook's passing potential was what provided the necessary momentum. "We were playing an inspired defense," he observed afterward, "and we had to be patient."

Many thought Brook would be distracted in that game because, for the first time in two months, Tommie Frazier was on the sideline in uniform, possibly ready to play–though he had not scrimmaged. In fact, it hadn't been decided that he'd be on the trip to Oklahoma until that Thursday morning, the day the Cornhuskers left for the game. Those who wondered what impact Frazier's presence might have on him didn't know Brook Berringer. He was made of sterner stuff than that. Through the heart of the schedule he had led his team to repeated victories. He had earned the starting role; and he knew that–for the moment at least–No. 15 was now his backup.

Frazier kept a low profile in his return to uniform, declining interview requests afterward.

As the regular season ended, the Big Red Machine began preparations for a return trip to the Orange Bowl and a crack at Miami to determine the national championship. Brook was the quarterback. Based on the way he was passing at season's end, he would have needed only one more game to move into Nebraska's single-season top 10 passers of all time. And if he'd had the opportunity to have played the full season, he might have finished in the top five.

Certainly Nebraska's defense had played superbly over the eight game stretch, holding the opposition to only 87 points. Meanwhile, in comparison, the offense, with some great rushing figures, racked up 243 points on the scoreboard. The outstanding play of Brook Berringer had also helped give the Cornhuskers a crack at the national title for a second year in a row. Ever since a narrow loss–by inches–in that same Orange Bowl against Florida State the previous New Year's Day, the Huskers, as a team, had been on a mission. They were unified under one theme–*unfinished business.*

Brook took time to squeeze in some precious hours of hunting after the Oklahoma game. Walking the fields with his dog and favorite hunting companion, Juke, was never time consuming for Brook. It was such a release to him in mind and spirit that he always had renewed vigor to accomplish that much more in other matters.

He wrapped up his studies for the semester and turned his major attention to preparation for Miami. Not only did he need to know everything he could about the Hurricanes, but once again there was serious competition for his place behind center Aaron Graham.

Cleared for contact by his doctor, Tommie Frazier was back practicing. However, Coach Osborne explained that Brook would be the likely starter, as he had been for seven of the last eight games, if Frazier wasn't able to play in the two planned team scrimmages before the bowl game: one in Lincoln and the second in Miami.

In mid-December at a Big Red Breakfast, Coach Osborne commented on Brook's season, "As coaches, we felt we had a player in Berringer who certainly was very good, but we weren't sure about his confidence. We weren't quite sure how he'd react when the heat was on. But we did know he was 6-4, 210, and could run a 4.6, and had a nice arm." Then, Osborne added, "He came through and played awfully well."

Many people, including normally well-informed sportswriters, thought it was a question of making a choice between two effective quarterbacks with contrasting styles. But that was not the case, nor has it ever been the case with an Osborne-coached team. His offensive approach to every game has never been based on who started at quarterback. (In two games when Brook was most vulnerable to re-injuring his lung, Nebraska did run fewer option plays.) It seemed to many people that Nebraska threw more passes with Brook at the helm, but that was not the case: he just had a high completion percentage (over 60) and many of his passes were for long yardage.

Brook always preferred a more wide-open offense, but that was never the case, and he knew that from the beginning. He also knew that this was a competitive situation, which he approached pragmatically. "I think it's a deal where they're going to start whoever is the best prepared."

In his heart, of course, he intended to be that man.

The coaches could do little to alleviate the tension created by the quarterback controversy. Fans, friends, and the press all wanted to know who would be the starting quarterback. In Miami, the results of the team scrimmage on December 24 were supposed to determine the starter. But even three days after that it was still up in the air. Coach Osborne did give a hint of his intentions when he said, "It may be that one of them will play most all the time and one a limited role. But I don't think it will be a deal where one guy stands there and watches the whole game." He went on to affirm that the player who graded the highest from the first pre-bowl practice would start; but that the other should not consider himself inferior.

If the decision was based on recent performance, Brook would come out on top. Frazier, sidelined since September 25, had rushed only once and completed one pass since September 17. Brook, on the other hand, had overcome all the detractors who hadn't given him a chance of success. "I came into a tough situation where a lot of people maybe had some question as to whether I'd be able to get it done," he said. "To most people who know anything about football, I think we've proven we can still move the football."

He had helped set the stage for the Cornhuskers to go into their final act ranked No. 1. To prove himself definitively in that contest was his burning desire. And to be the starter was mighty important also.

However, that was not to be.

At Nebraska, everyone knows that a starter can't lose his position due to injury. Also, Tommie had been the starter for two previous bowl games. As difficult as it was for Brook to accept a secondary role, he knew Coach Osborne's decision was fair. There are plenty of athletes in society today that can't handle a supporting role on a team–especially if they've been in the spotlight before. But for Brook it was simply a matter of being a team player.

CHAPTER 7

ORANGE BOWL 1994—A CHAMPIONSHIP

Though replaced by Tommie Frazier, Brook hoped in his heart he would get a chance to prove himself. Despite much praise (and occasional criticism) during the long stretch of the season, he had done an admirable job of staying focused and steady. "Give this team the credit," he said. "It's not important if they give me any credit because that's not what it's all about for me. I'm going to have fun and do my part to make sure we win a national title.

"All the rest of the talk really doesn't matter."

In saying that, Brook was expressing the basic truth of his heart—the success of his team was far more important to him than any personal goal. Yet, at the same time, he affirmed, "I never set a goal to be a backup quarterback." That was not his mode of participation in any part of life. He was a competitor. He knew within himself that he had the tools to be a good quarterback and was willing to pay whatever price that took to prove it. His statistics for the 1994 season had begun to impress people, as though he had come out of nowhere.

But all of that was ancient history as Brook headed to the stadium in Miami with the rest of the team on January 1, 1995. The claim to the national championship was on the line.

Brook was questioned by the media for weeks on what some in the press hoped would become a controversial quarterback wrangle. Brook stated simply, definitively, "I expect to play, and play well."

Truly, that is all he wanted for himself.

But more important than that, he wanted Nebraska to win the game. "I'm not so worried about myself," he declared honestly, "as I am about making sure we win another game. I don't think it matters who comes in, when, or why–we're both capable of getting the job done." He steadfastly refused to badmouth his counterpart at quarterback. Likewise, Tommie refused to get into any negative speculation either.

It had been 98 days, from September 24, since Frazier had played in a ball game. He had kept himself in good physical shape, and Coach Osborne's intuition pointed in his favor.

Nebraska's first possession with Frazier behind center was rusty–three and out, along with a time out before the second snap.

Miami's first possession wasn't impressive, but a field goal gave them a 3-0 lead.

A combination of Hurricane penalties and a good running game produced three first downs for the Cornhuskers on their next offensive series. But an interception of a Frazier pass at the 3-yard line turned the ball back to Miami.

Behind the strong arm of Frank Costa, Miami drove the length of the field, 97 yards, to gain a 10-0 advantage with seven seconds left in the first quarter.

Enter Brook Berringer. His first hand-off to Lawrence Phillips was good for a 15-yard gain and a first down, but the series ended with a 5-yard sack and a punt.

Miami punted back, leaving Nebraska with decent field position.

Two carries by Phillips were good for 10 yards and a first down, followed by a great 9-yard carry by Riley Washington. The NBC announcers were in agreement that, "Berringer was giving the offense a lift. Just the threat of his passing ability was enough to open up the running game." As if taking a cue from that, after another short run for a first down, Brook hit Mark Gilman for a 19-yard touchdown pass on a play-action fake.

Nebraska was on the scoreboard, back in the game at 10-7.

Although the Huskers managed two first downs in the next two possessions, both teams were forced to punt twice before heading to the locker room for halftime.

Miami struck quickly in the second half. In just a minute, 41 seconds, the Hurricanes took the kickoff, then swept down the field, and completed the drive with a touchdown pass from Costa.

17-7, Miami.

Nebraska's first possession went nowhere, three and out. But the punt left Miami deep and an aggressive defense and two penalties pushed the Canes inside the 5-yard line. Nebraska's linebacker Dwayne Harris then wrapped Costa in his arms in the end zone for a safety.

17-9, Miami.

Nebraska bobbled the ball on the ensuing kickoff, but had the ball on the 25-yard line. Phillips ran for 3, Brook passed for 7–first down. Fullback Cory Schlesinger ran for 5 and Phillips for 3, then, taking too much time, the Cornhuskers were hit with a 5-yard delay of game penalty.

On the next play, a shovel pass fell incomplete and Nebraska had to punt.

Miami started an impressive drive, but after three first downs they had to punt.

Nebraska took the ball on the 6-yard line. Schlesinger and Phillips ran for 7 yards each. Then Brook hit Abdul Muhammad for 16 yards, and after Phillips was thrown for a 3-yard loss, Brook hit Muhammad with another 19-yard pass. Again after short losses by Phillips and Brook, Brook let loose another 15-yard pass to Muhammad. On fourth and one, Brook plunged in behind his big center Aaron Graham for the first down. A lob pass to Phillips made Brook four-for-four on the drive. But a poor handoff on the next play led to a fumble and Miami took over as the third quarter came to an end.

Miami was three and out on its first possession of the quarter and fumbled the snap on the punt attempt. Nebraska had the ball first and goal on the 4-yard line, and Coach Osborne sent in a pass play. Mark Gilman was open momentarily, but under pressure Brook rolled out to his right. Realizing he'd held onto the ball a second too long, he tried to throw it out of the end zone but it was intercepted by inches. Immediately he squeezed his helmet with both hands, wishing he had heaved the ball just a yard further.

A touchdown and a two-point conversion would have tied the game–but.

Once again, Miami couldn't move the ball–three-and-out, punt.

Now that Miami's defense was wearing down, Coach Osborne sent Tommie Frazier back in the game hoping to take advantage of his ability to make big plays with 12:07 left in the game. In Tommie's first series back in the game, he was sacked for a loss of six, passed for 13 to Muhammad, was thrown for a loss on an option keeper, and Nebraska had to punt.

For a third time, Miami was three-and-out, punt as Nebraska continued to play outstanding defense.

Now Nebraska had great field position on the 40-yard line. Phillips immediately broke loose for a 30-yard romp and Schlesinger followed with a 15-yard burst into the end zone. On a Frazier two-point conversion pass to Alford, Nebraska tied the game at 17-17. Along the sidelines, Brook's face lit up with a smile of approval.

On the ensuing kickoff with 6:28 to play in the game, unbelievably, the power offense of the Hurricanes once again sputtered–three-and-out, punt. Nebraska's strategy of wearing down the Hurricanes in the fourth quarter worked to perfection.

Nebraska picked up two first downs with Phillips carrying the ball three times, Frazier gaining big yardage on two third down runs, and a 7-yard Frazier to Reggie Baul pass. Then the unsung hero of the game, Cory Schlesinger, refusing to be stopped, plunged into the end zone for his second touchdown of the quarter.

It was Nebraska, 24-17.

Working from its own 17-yard line, Miami suffered two monstrous sacks of its quarterback and a final desperation heave on fourth down which was intercepted on the 50-yard line. This play turned the ball and the national championship over to Nebraska.

Tommie Frazier was named the Orange Bowl's Most Valuable Player for helping Nebraska overcome Miami's lead in the fourth quarter. Brook's 8-of-15 passing for 81 yards and a touchdown also contributed to Nebraska's first national championship under Coach Tom Osborne.

As pandemonium reigned in the Cornhuskers' dressing room after the game, Brook was as ecstatic as anyone. He knew he had made a valuable contribution to the game. His team was the national champion of college football. And the operative word for him was "team." Yes, his contribution of starting and winning seven games was somewhat lost in the light of the moment, but he knew what he'd done; and he was deeply satisfied.

"We both have nothing to hang our heads about," Brook said afterward. "We both made some mistakes. We both made some good plays. We both helped our team win."

CHAPTER 8

HOPES FOR 1995

From the moment of the last bits of praise in the Orange Bowl, sportswriters began a steady drumbeat to arouse a controversy as to who would be the Cornhuskers' starting quarterback for 1995. The question was swirling so constantly that, at a mini news conference two months ahead of spring drills, Brook and Tommie took turns talking to a group of writers.

The interesting thing about that session was that the reporters were asking the wrong questions of the wrong men. Coach Osborne wasn't there. Trying to get into the heads of two young quarterbacks might have helped them fill up empty newspaper columns with trivia for their readers, but the answer to who would be the starting quarterback was in the coach. Anyone who has been around Nebraska football knows that Osborne has a set policy that no starter can lose his position due to injury, which would seem to ensure Frazier of being the starter.

Nonetheless, Brook had true hope for the next season. "This is the first time I feel like I have a legitimate shot at being the starter next year," he said. "It's a confidence that you get from playing with the top units. I know what I'm doing. I've got the offense down pat. That takes the pressure off and builds confidence."

He further explained the difficulty in previous years of trying to establish himself at Nebraska, "I remember playing with a sixth-team guard at center (in practice), and he wasn't sure which hand to snap with. There's nothing that destroys your confidence faster than that."

That problem of not playing with first-string personnel had plagued him in all the action he saw in his first two seasons. The only exception to that was the opening game of the year against North Texas as a sophomore, when Frazier went out in the first quarter with an ankle injury. The subtle differences he experienced playing behind a variety of different centers could result in a major miscue when split-second timing is all important. At Nebraska, there is no shortage of talented linemen. But it's always a bit difficult for the quarterback and center to adjust to one another. Brook was always sensitive to that irregularity. "Of course, I was a bit frustrated," he admitted, "but that's only natural. No one had ever seen me play. I always said if a chance ever comes up, I'll be ready."

For the 1995 season, however, he didn't anticipate that problem. He fully expected to be surrounded by top-unit players.

Reflecting on the 1994 season, Brook observed that one major reason the change in quarterbacks worked for the Cornhuskers was the reaction of the whole squad. "The team stayed focused and the quarterback situation—through Tommie's injury, my injury, Matt's shoulder injury against Missouri—didn't seem to bother the team at all. It would've been easy for guys to have some doubt about me. For them to wonder, 'Who's this guy?' But there was none of that all season."

On the contrary, the steady support he received from his teammates built fresh assurance in Brook himself. "Sometimes," he explained, "when a guy comes from a small high school, confidence is a factor." (His Goodland High School senior-year experience was with a 5-4 football team.) "I didn't have confidence.

"It wasn't Tommie's fault that he got hurt, and it wasn't my fault that I played well. I had a chance to start in seven games, and I played well enough. Tommie came back, won the starting job back, and together, with the whole team, we won the national championship."

With that said, Brook took a no-nonsense approach to prepare for spring ball. During the winter conditioning period, he added another 10 pounds of muscle strength to his 6-foot-4 frame, up to

220 pounds. The payoff to that effort came during the team's physical testing in mid-March. He posted an all-time record for the quarterback position at 2,547 points in the performance index, which measures athleticism based on weight. The highlight was an electronic 4.63-second time in the 40-yard dash.

What really fueled him through January and February was his belief that he had a real chance to earn the starting job at quarterback. "I've always felt like if you work hard and want something bad enough you can make it come true. All I wanted was a chance to prove I could do it. Now I feel like the coaches are a lot more confident in me because they know I can get the job done."

Still he didn't think the coaches owed him anything. Though he felt he had proven himself, he knew he'd have to prove himself again. And he looked forward to competition, knowing that it would make him even better. "Maybe at times a guy tends to relax a little bit in practice," he said, "especially if he's No. 2. Neither one of us can afford to do that now.

"Not that we were ever lazy, but once in a while you're thinking, 'Maybe I don't need to go full speed on this play, so I'm not going to run the fake out 20 yards.' Now both of us are going to be working as hard as we can."

Though focused on being well-prepared for spring ball, Brook, as he had for 14 years, slipped out into the countryside for hunting several mornings a week. In doing so, he reaped his favorite benefit of fame. "It's helpful," he said, "to be recognized when you stop at a farmer's place to get on a good place to hunt."

On one occasion, near Hickman, a farmer was about to drive to town when Brook and a friend pulled up to ask about hunting. When the man saw him he turned and ran to get his wife and her camera. "Do you mind if we hunt in your fields?" Brook asked.

"I knew you were going to ask when I saw you get out of your truck," the farmer replied. "Of course, I don't mind. But if you'll take the time for my wife to get a picture of us, I'll lead you out beyond the barn to the best huntin' ground in Lancaster County."

Brook never turned down a request for a picture, and he figured hunting privileges were a good payment. He posed all smiles with the burly farmer, then went off to bag his limit of quail.

Later, in a similar situation near Crete, Brook attracted even more attention. The farmer who owned the land where Brook and his house mate Brad were hunting quail called his neighbor to secure permission to cross onto his property, explaining that the Cornhuskers' quarterback was there. When they entered the adjacent field they saw several pickup trucks stop along the road. Brook's first thought was that there was going to be a complaint.

"We thought we were in trouble," Brad said, "because when someone is mad at you for being on their land, they'll usually drive out and get you."

But as they got near the trucks, six or seven people with posters, banners, and other Nebraska football paraphernalia got out and rushed toward Brook. Instead of a controversy, an autograph signing session commenced right there in the cornfield. As always, Brook took it in stride, signing for everybody.

At the same time, Brad was relieved. "Here I thought it was the game warden, and it was a bunch of football fans."

Brook was even becoming somewhat of a celebrity in his hometown. When he returned home from the Orange Bowl game against Miami, Brook found a stack of items a foot high on the dining room table to be signed. Local fans had dropped them off for Brook to autograph when he came back to Goodland. Brook took time to sign each of the items.

Jan's fourth grade students also saw value in Brook's signature and would give her little slips of paper to take with her for Brook to sign for them after the games. While she was drinking from a souvenir cup at one of the games, she got the idea to have Brook sign cups for her students instead of the tiny scraps of paper. She began taking a plastic bag in her purse to home games so she could collect discarded cups after the game.

"Mom! Don't go around picking up cups!" Brook complained. "You look like a bag lady. You're probably going to get on some TV camera picking up cups after the game!"

"Brook, these are for the kids. I don't care what it looks like," was Jan's reply.

She would collect enough cups for both fourth grade classes and then run them through the dishwasher three times. After Brook signed each one, she would put in a Nebraska sticker and pencil, and pass them out to the students. The students loved the gift and were careful not to wash the cup in the dishwasher for fear that Brook's autograph might come off. Older brothers and sisters even offered to buy the cups from these young students but this treasure was one thing that money could not buy.

Before the start of spring practice it was evident that Coach Osborne was keeping his own thoughts confidential on the question of who would start behind center. He explained that Brook and Tommie would have equal time with the No. 1 unit during the 15 practice sessions, "They'll probably get equal snaps in scrimmages. Whoever comes out of spring ball grading the best will start out No. 1 in the fall.

"But we'll still have 29 practices, including three pretty good scrimmages in the fall. So that's subject to change."

The controversy, which media people would have loved to report, never developed into a visible duel. Osborne continually downplayed the competition by referring the press to his point system for quarterbacks.

Each play is graded on a point system. Two points are awarded for simply running the play correctly. If a quarterback turns the wrong way, makes the wrong audible or is the reason a play broke down, that's one point. And interceptions or fumbles are zero points.

The points are then added and each quarterback is given an average after each practice or scrimmage. The point averages accumulate over the spring and fall. Typically, the higher average means that man earns the job on consistency or lack of mistakes. Of course, no system is perfect or pleases everyone.

In the all-important annual Red-White intrasquad scrimmage on April 22, as expected, the battle for starting quarterback honors dominated the scrimmage.

Tommie made his case early in the scrimmage, completing 5 of 13 passes for 228 yards and two touchdowns. He also gained 14 yards and another touchdown on five rushing attempts. In the process, he made some mental mistakes and a couple of turnovers.

Brook also had a stellar afternoon, completing 3 of 6 passes for 62 yards, including a 41-yard toss to a wide-open Mark Gilman on the Red team's first offensive series. He also broke loose on an option keeper for a 36-yard touchdown.

According to the point system, Frazier held a slim lead. Osborne said both would continue to be graded in scrimmages before the August 31 season opener at Oklahoma State. "The top quarterback will be the starter," he promised, "and the other will also play in the first half."

Brook appreciated the fact that Osborne had taken the heat out of the situation, "He's done a good job of not making a big deal of it. It's not something that gets out of hand because of the way he's dealing with it. However," he added with a smile, "it'd be nice to give this all a rest and just play football. We know we have to try hard, give our best and the rest will take care of itself."

With the conclusion of the spring semester, Brook busied himself in traveling around the state as an ambassador for the athletic department, speaking in various situations. He was especially pleased with the opportunities to bring encouragement into hospital wards and nursing homes. His own memories of having to hunt for Easter eggs on the hospital lawn while his dad received treatments for his cancer were all too vivid for Brook. Since he would do almost anything to avoid being a patient in a hospital, he cherished those moments of lifting the spirits of others.

In late June, Brook spent part of a Tuesday afternoon at Immanuel Medical Center in Omaha. One of the kids he saw, James Katskee, was a bit groggy as he had been medicated for surgery. But his father, looking on approvingly said, "He'll be really excited to know that the quarterback of the Huskers was here just ahead of his surgery."

"He's going to think I'm a bad side effect of the morphine," Brook replied with a laugh.

Two weeks before fall camp (on the heels of moving to a new house), a few days of muskie fishing was Brook's last planned break of the summer. He was determined to be in good shape for the physically demanding two-a-day practices.

Quarterback Coach Turner Gill insisted to the media that he was maintaining a neutral position to the controversy. "We have a couple of guys who can win. They can come from behind. They can protect a lead. They'll compete, and they'll be better than either one was a year ago. They both know that, and they both know the team comes first."

In the first team scrimmage, the second Sunday of August, Coach Osborne said his top two quarterbacks graded "dead-even." Though slowed by a sore hamstring, Brook took 14 snaps and completed 4 of 6 passes for 44 yards. In 21 plays, Frazier was 3-for-10 for 57 yards with 2 touchdowns and an interception.

But Brook understood the meaning behind "dead-even." That meant Frazier was still ahead because coach intended to factor in the spring points. To be the starter, he would have to perform at near perfection. That was his heart's desire, but he also knew history. During three years in uniform he had started just seven games, Frazier more than 20. "If coach has any preference," he reasoned, "it has to be in favor of the one he has called on the most." Even to Brook, it made sense that Coach Osborne in a "dead-even" situation would give the nod to Tommie because of his experience and exceptional talents. After all, he was "the only true freshman ever to start at quarterback for Nebraska."

That knowledge served to spur Brook all the more to achieve the goal. For the first time in four years in Lincoln, the coaches were assuring him that he had a chance to open the season as the starter at quarterback.

"I just hope I get a chance to show what I can do," he said.

CHAPTER 9

DISAPPOINTMENT AND GAIN

Thursday, August 24, was a day Brook had worked toward for months–or in a sense for all his life. The final preseason scrimmage had been held the previous afternoon and his play had been stellar–6 of 8 passes completed for 118 yards and one touchdown, four rushes for minus one yard. Frazier's statistics were almost identical: 7 of 8 passes for 125 yards and one TD, two rushes for minus four yards. From that three-and-a-half hour trial, the head coach and the quarterback coach met together to average out the points they assessed; and from that they would have to determine a starting quarterback for the year.

As he dressed for classes that morning, Brook sensed his dad's presence in a special way on a doubly special day. It was Warren and William's birthday. How he wished his dad were with him to help hold him steady if the coaches' decision was not in his favor. But he pushed aside any negative thoughts; he knew he had a chance at being the starter against Oklahoma State.

Throughout the day he held on to that thought.

But it was not to be.

Brook first learned of the decision in the theater-style team meeting room on the second floor of South Stadium. To Brook, it seemed as though the name "Frazier" was amplified throughout the room, tier upon tier.

When he heard the declaration from the coach, he felt an emptiness in the pit of his stomach. He tried hard not to let his head sag or change his facial expression. He bit his inner lip and stared straight ahead; disappointment churned in his gut. He tried to focus his thoughts far away from that room. He thought of a happy moment many years distant, his dad's last birthday celebration when he himself was only seven.

With that he was able to crack a bit of a smile. But it still hurt.

Nonetheless, for a competitor like Brook who always strove with all his heart to be his best, it's an especially painful experience not to come out on top. His only comment to the press was, "My attitude this year is that it's going to be important that both of us get a chance to play. In my eyes, it's not who starts but who finishes. If I don't finish, then I'll be disappointed by the end."

Brook knew how, through years of practice, to hold his emotions in check and put a decent face on everything. Yet his disappointment burned deeply. He had been edged out of a starting position that he thought he should have won.

After Brook had called his very close family friend, Jim McKee, to discuss the disappointing news, he then called home to tell his mother that Tommie had gotten the nod. "Well, Brook. It's not a total surprise, is it?" Jan asked. "You did everything you could do–and that's all you can ask of yourself. You have proven yourself, Brook. You've proven yourself to the coaches, to the fans and most important to you. So don't worry about it. Maybe by standing on the sidelines you can save yourself for the NFL."

Brook's frustration was normal. Who wouldn't have felt disappointed at failing to reach their goals? He had spent years of his life working toward this moment–now it was passing without anything he could do or say. He had done everything that was expected of him, but he still came up short. He had been the consummate team player.

Brook could easily have created a scene that would have divided the team. And he knew that many fans would sympathize with his dilemma. But Brook knew that wouldn't have been right.

It was at this point in Brook's life, when he felt he hadn't got what he deserved, that God used me, Art Lindsay, to share a message of hope.

I met Brook through a mutual friend–Receivers Coach Ron Brown. I admired Brook based on what I heard about him. In fact, during the year prior to our first meeting, I prayed for him regularly, sensing God's desire to use him in a significant way. But it wasn't until I was able to spend some time with him to encourage him spiritually that I realized just how special Brook was.

It was exciting to discover while putting this book together that Warren, Brook's father, had an incredibly strong faith and that he and Jan together had established a very strong spiritual heritage.

"Once, when Warren was in the hospital, he was having an especially difficult time," explained Jan's sister Jolene. "He had been allowed to take two items into a specially sterilized cancer treatment room. His Bible was the only one he chose. In his despair, Warren started reading about the crucifixion of Jesus and it suddenly dawned on him that Jesus had gone through all that suffering just for him."

After reading that passage, Warren told Jolene, "If God can be glorified in my suffering, then that is all I want. You know, Jo, for the first time since I can remember I actually feel happy on the inside."

It was that experience, and Jan's persistence in the following years, that helped provide the foundation Brook needed for a relationship with God. Faith was important to both of his parents, and Jan saw to it that Brook attended church to hear God's Word, and the two talked often about spiritual matters. However, decisions of faith are made individually, and while the foundation was there, actually trusting Christ with his life was a decision Brook had not seemingly dealt with yet.

As had been our habit for several weeks, the best time to get together was on Thursday evening at 9:15. That August 24th had been a full day on my schedule, capped by an evening with inmates at the Lincoln Correctional Center, where I do a volunteer ministry, and I had not gone home before heading for Brook's house.

If I had, events would have turned out differently. As it was, when I heard a blip of the sports news on the car radio that Tommie, not Brook, was chosen as the starting quarterback, I was especially anxious to see him so I could encourage him.

Brook never did put on a front for me. When I walked into his house, the normal smile of greeting was absent. "Didn't you get my message?" he asked. "I can't meet with you tonight."

I had never seen him look so depressed.

"No," I answered, "I haven't been home all day."

I knew how he must be hurting, but I didn't want to put words in his mouth so I asked simply, "What's up?"

"I suppose you heard," he replied sadly, "Coach chose Frazier to be starting quarterback."

"Yes," I admitted in empathetic tone. "I've been out at the Correctional Center all evening, but heard it a few minutes ago on the radio." I searched desperately for an encouraging word, but I could think of none, knowing he would have detested anything trite.

Finally, I said, "I don't know what the outcome of this will be, but I know that God is going to use it in your life . . . He will prove Himself to you.

"I'm so certain that God intends to use your life dramatically that I want to ask you right now for the privilege of helping you write a book about your life."

Brook responded, "Not right now, but someday."

As his house mate Brad passed through the living room, and headed for the kitchen, Brook suggested, "Let's go outside to talk."

We sat down on the top step of the front porch and I repeated my previous observation, "Brook, I know this is a great disappointment for you because you've worked so hard, but God wants to bless you in it. Have you ever heard Romans 8:28 in the Bible?"

"No," he replied.

Opening my Bible, I said, "This is one of the greatest promises ever written." Showing him the verse, I read,

"And we know that in all things God works for the good of those who love him, who have been called according to his purpose."

"The real key to this," I went on, "is whether or not you love Him.

"Now, I know you love God," I followed up quickly, "but I mean in terms of a personal relationship where you've allowed Him control of your life.

"I've suggested to you twice in the last few weeks that you should pray on your own and accept Jesus Christ in your life."

I paused a moment before asking, "Have you done that?"

With a sincerity wrapped in humility he answered directly, "Art, I've never understood what that really means."

"Then may I take the time right now to explain it?" I asked.

"Certainly!" he answered. Instantly, the humiliation of the afternoon faded in the light of a desire to gain an eternal perspective. Intent upon getting to the bottom of this matter, he now had all the time in the world for me.

"Really, my friend, the plan of salvation that God offers us is quite simple. Theologians and philosophers get lost in high sounding phrases, but for you and me, God simply wants to establish a relationship with us–a Father/son relationship. It's expressed best in John 3:16," I said, turning to that passage.

"For God so loved the world, that he gave his one and only Son, that whoever believes in him shall not perish but have eternal life."

"You see, Brook, it's not because of anything that you and I have done to deserve eternal life. Rather it's because God loves us that He sent Jesus Christ to be our Savior. See, just above here, in the seventh verse is where Jesus instructs us, 'You must be born again.' "

Brook placed his index finger on the page, and studied the surrounding verses. "So, is this where that expression comes from?" he asked.

"Yes," I replied, "but you and I have a great problem that holds us back from being 'born again.' You see, sin separates us from God."

I turned to Romans 3:23 and read as Brook followed along,

"For all have sinned and fall short of the glory of God."

"That verse lumps you and me and everyone who has ever lived in one category–sinners. It doesn't matter whether our sins have been big or little, we still fall short of God's best. Does that make sense?"

"Yes," he nodded.

"It's because of our sins that you and I are faced with a big problem."

I turned a page in the Bible. "Romans 6:23 tells us clearly,

'For the wages of sin is death . . .' "

As I paused, Brook looked up from reading; I could sense that he was discovering a truth that would change his life forever.

"All Art Lindsay or Brook Berringer deserve," I continued, "is death and hell. But as you saw from the conclusion of that verse,

'. . . but the gift of God is eternal life in Christ Jesus our Lord.'

"Because of His great love for us as expressed in John 3:16, knowing that because of our sins we could never earn our way into eternal life, God devised a simple plan of salvation. He would just give it outright to anyone who would accept it.

"Romans 10:9 then expresses for us the conditions."

Again I read aloud as Brook followed along,

"That if you confess with your mouth, 'Jesus is Lord,' and believe in your heart that God raised him from the dead, you will be saved."

"Man, I know you've heard about Jesus all your life. But in order to obtain that relationship for yourself you have to personalize it; you have to internalize it.

"And there's one final verse of scripture I want to show you that tells exactly how you and I can do that, 1 John 1:9."

I turned the pages to near the end of the Bible and Brook read,

"If we confess our sins, he is faithful and just and will forgive us our sins and purify us from all unrighteousness."

"Brook," I advised him, closing the Bible and holding it firmly in my right hand, "this book is our source of authority; and it's not difficult to understand. From cover to cover, God tells us in many different ways and in the life situations of all kinds of people, that He loves us and has a wonderful plan for our lives.

"All it takes," I said, holding up the index finger of my left hand, "is to recognize that you have a sin problem that you can do nothing about, and that God has the only solution.

"Then," as I raised my other index finger and hooked it into the first one, "as you place your faith in that free gift of love from God you form an unbreakable relationship with Him."

I tugged hard at my interlocked fingers.

"Does that make sense?" I asked.

"Yes," he smiled, "I understand exactly what you're saying."

"Would you like to pray about it right now, and ask Jesus to come into your heart?" I asked hopefully.

"Yes, I would," he responded without hesitation.

I looked him squarely in the eye and said, "Brook, I don't care what sins you've ever committed. From my perspective, I've never seen any. But you don't have to confess any sins to me. God is the one you have to talk to. Okay?"

"Okay," he replied

After I had prayed aloud and concluded with an amen, Brook continued with his head bowed for awhile. Finally he turned to me with a fresh contentment on his face.

"Is it all settled between you and God then?" I asked.

"Yes, thank you," he assured me.

Time was running short because of a study group for a business class he had to go to so I turned quickly to a practical matter. I asked, "Do you have a study Bible of your own?"

"Not really," he answered.

"Okay, I'll order one for you and have it for you next week."

"Will you get one for Tiffini, too?" he asked immediately, referring to his girlfriend.

"Gladly," I assured him. "Now in the meantime, I want you to take mine so you can restudy these verses on your own, then we'll go over them again next week."

On a scrap of paper he wrote down those life-changing references.

"Let's get together Tuesday night next week," Brook suggested. "The Oklahoma State game is down there next Thursday."

"Great," I agreed. "And don't forget, I pray for you continually."

"Thanks, and I pray for you, too," he smiled as he turned to go into the house.

What an interesting parallel in dates that Warren Berringer was *born* on August 24, and that half a century later Brook Warren Berringer was *born again* on August 24.

Brook paused as he got into his truck to drive to his study group. He got out and went back into the house to get the Bible. "I need to see those verses again," he determined.

Sitting alone, using the index to find his way through the Book, he chewed on each verse again briefly. As they all fit together so perfectly, a deep contentment lodged in his spirit–his commitment of himself to Christ was the most important decision of the day, of his life.

The next week when I met with Brook, I talked to him about studying a new playbook.

"Let me ask you, when you came to the University of Nebraska how many of the football plays did you know in the Cornhuskers' playbook?"

"I didn't know any," he answered.

"How many do you know now?" I continued.

"I know them all," he declared with certainty.

"So," I said, "when Coach calls a play, you run down to the locker room, get out your playbook, look up the play, hurry back on the field, and run the play."

"No," he responded firmly, in tune with the scenario I was laying out. "When Coach calls a play I run it!"

I picked up his new Bible that I had just given him from where he'd laid it on the top step and said, "Brook! This is your Playbook. You have to know this *book* better than you know the University of Nebraska playbook."

"Okay," he nodded in agreement, the excitement of a new adventure evident in his eyes, "How do I get started?"

For emphasis I used the old Navigator illustration of the hand as the total method of gaining knowledge of the Word of God. The first three fingers, representing hearing, reading, even studying the Word are not sufficient. "As you know from football, the only way to remember a hundred percent of anything is to memorize it.

"That's the fourth finger," I said as I showed that I could get a rather strong grip using just the four fingers.

"But knowledge without application is worthless." I continued, "You have to get into the game. That's the thumb of the hand. That's what gives you the grip. As you learn the Word of God, you have to put it into practice."

I gripped his Bible firmly with my whole hand to illustrate the effect. "Now I have such control of the Word, that even a big guy like you couldn't get it away from me."

He smiled in understanding agreement.

"Does that make sense at all?" I asked.

"Yes," he answered. Then, with enthusiasm, he asked the question, "Where do I start? In the Book of Genesis?"

"In order to get a real foundation of what you've experienced personally, I suggest you start studying in the Gospel of John which describes our relationship with Christ in vital terms. Genesis will come later.

"But in order to get the Playbook memorized, I think you need to start with the verses we went through last Thursday. That way, in the future, when you want to help someone else know how to come into a relationship with Christ, you'll know the simple plan by heart.

"I've put them in my computer for you and printed out your first list. Between now and next Tuesday I want you to get these basic verses in your memory bank."

Brook took the sheet of paper entitled "Brook's Memory Bank." The following verses were listed:

> John 3:16
> Romans 3:23
> Romans 6:23
> Romans 10:9
> 2 Corinthians 5:17
> 1 John 1:9

"As you see," I observed, "I slipped in a verse we haven't talked about before, 2 Corinthians 5:17."

Turning to it in his Bible, I continued, "I added it because it describes you, what took place in your life last week."

Brook studied the words with deep interest,

> "Therefore, if anyone is in Christ, he is a new creation; the
> old has gone, the new has come!"

As he read it over several times he internalized it. At once it became his favorite verse because it described in simple words what was so otherwise inexpressible.

Brook had recognized his need for Christ, and gave God control of his life. As a new creation, he was now set to experience the peace and joy that nothing–including a starting role as quarterback–could bring.

CHAPTER *10*

GREATEST SEASON OF ALL

Though disappointed at not being named the starting quarterback, Brook went off to Stillwater, Oklahoma, for the August 31 opener with a new perspective and hope for a good season. The plan the coaches had set up was that, "Frazier will play the first two or three series, then Berringer."

Unfortunately, it didn't work out that way. Oklahoma State played tough defense for the first quarter, and only a 3-yard touchdown run by Lawrence Phillips gave Nebraska a 6-0 lead.

Brook didn't get into the game until nearly the half. Once on the field, however, he took full advantage of the limited playing time he was afforded. Brook completed 6 of 11 passes for 106 yards, which would turn out to be his best total of the season.

The next game was at Michigan State in East Lansing. He was excited that there was going to be a big Berringer contingent in the stands. He had scraped together more than 30 tickets to satisfy requests from family members and friends including the Sawyer-Brown country group (with whom Brook had become quite close) and his Aunt Jolene and Uncle Stan's family from Indiana and Michigan. Uncle Willie and Aunt Judy also made the trip, as they did all of Brook's games his senior season. Little did they know when they made plans to go that it would be, due to a leg injury of Frazier, his most extensive action of the entire season.

It was a brilliant afternoon for football; the sun had driven away most of the morning chill, and there wasn't a cloud in the sky.

Though outnumbered, of course, there were large sections of Nebraska fans in the far corners of the Spartans' stadium, with an abundance of red sprinkled throughout the stands.

The highlight of the game for Brook, and his favorite of the whole season, was a perfect 51-yard toss to Reggie Baul, who stretched out almost flat to catch the pass. After a quick score into the end zone on the next two plays, the sidelines were rampant with congratulations to Brook, who beamed with smiles of satisfaction. With him in command for nearly three-quarters of the game, Nebraska came away with an impressive 50-10 victory. Not only the Berringer block, but a whole section of Cornhuskers fans in the northeast corner of the stands stood in ovation as he and others left the field.

Brook joyously looked toward family and friends and raised his helmet high in silent salute back to them.

When we talked the next night, back in Lincoln, Brook was genuinely satisfied with his performance, since Nebraska held only a slim 13-10 lead when he was sent into the game cold. Once again he felt he had proven himself; and that is all he ever wanted. The pain of watching from the sidelines in the early part of any game was always a tense, tough test; though being a team player, he cheered every success of whoever was on the field.

After covering the highlights of the game (and laughing about the sportscaster who, in trying to add color commentary to the game, referred to him as a *"fisher* and hunter"), he abruptly changed the subject to Lawrence Phillips.

"I can't believe he'd give up so much," Brook said with anguish in his voice. "There went the Heisman . . . probably millions in the NFL."

There were no easy answers as to why a star running back like Phillips would allegedly assault his former girlfriend on the heels of the brilliant game he had played in Michigan. Though he was much closer in friendship with other players on the team like Phil Ellis, Clester Johnson, Tony Veland, Matt Turman and Chad Stanley, he had a genuine regard for Lawrence Phillips and was in a dilemma as to what this assault charge would do to him. He was equally troubled by the act itself. He was so attuned to the inner hurts of others that he couldn't imagine bringing intentional pain to anyone. That inner sensitivity drove him continually to put the concern of others ahead of his own.

"Brook," I said at last, "of course there's nothing we can do about it, but we can allow God to use it in our lives. Even a negative can be a great lesson. You and I are so blessed because we have so many resources of love and support from family and friends. But we're not yet all the men God wants us to be. When we see something like this it should be a reminder to focus all the more of our attention on Christ."

The Lawrence Phillips story so galvanized the attention of the media that Brook's splendid play at Michigan State was lost behind the Phillips headlines. That was still true the next two weeks as Nebraska entertained two opponents at home, Arizona State and Pacific.

After his performance at East Lansing, it was hard for Brook to watch the Arizona State game from the sidelines, especially with a lopsided score of 77-28. But he patiently plodded along the sideline with his sidekick Matt Turman, always a few feet away from the quarterback coach, Turner Gill.

The following week, as they were dressing in their room at the Nebraska Center, Brook quipped to Matt, "They won't need us against Pacific. They wouldn't even miss us. Turman, let's go fishing."

Matt roared in laughter. Then Brook broke up also.

But Brook and Matt headed for team chapel.

In the game itself, Brook had a season high rushing with 21 yards and was 9 for 17 passing for 57 yards.

For many college athletes, driven by desire for recognition, especially when they are gifted and talented, being relegated to second place would drive them to bitterness. But not Brook Berringer! Now more than ever, because of his faith in Christ he was able to handle pain, insults, broken hopes and recycle it all into an outlet of blessing to others.

Brook never sought the limelight. And, though he did attain it, he never flaunted it.

Purposely he chose not to go to some interviews requested of him. He seemed to have a sense ahead of time whether the reporter in question was merely trying to *make* a story. He refused to be a part of such contrivance.

On the other hand, much of what he did for others went unreported. He didn't know the teaching of Jesus, "Do not let your left hand know what your right hand is doing." (Matthew 6:3) But he put it into practice. He never tooted his own horn.

Yes, thousands have seen the video pictures of Brook visiting in a hospital ward. What they didn't know was that it was not just a rare "photo op" occasion. In June of 1995, on a visit at the Madonna Rehabilitation Hospital in Lincoln, he told Rob White of the *Omaha World-Herald*, "I feel like it's my duty as an athlete and as a role model. I've enjoyed my career here and the people of Nebraska have helped make it so enjoyable. It feels good giving something back to the community."

The reporter was on the scene for that scheduled appearance. But without any fanfare and without any camera flashes, on many occasions Brook would be passing a hospital and have a half-an-hour to spare. Knowing the loneliness of so many inside and sensing their need, he'd park his pickup truck, go inside to the receptionist's desk and introduce himself, "I'm Brook Berringer, a quarterback for Nebraska, and I wondered if there's anyone here who could use a visit from me."

Hospital staff usually, with great pleasure, took him in to the children's ward. He was never long on words. "Hey, how're you doin'?" was generally enough to raise the spirits of anyone. Then he'd sign all sorts of papers laid before him, arm and leg casts, and be gone.

No one called the newspaper, radio, or television reporters. The only ones who knew about such times were the lives he touched and Brook himself. And that's just the way he wanted it.

As the 1995 season progressed, many people wondered how

Brook really felt about being a backup quarterback after having started for most of the previous year. He answered that rather thoroughly in a radio interview with Lincoln sportscaster Bill Doleman.

"My career definitely has not been one of those where a guy comes in as a freshman and starts for four years. But it hasn't been, on the other hand, one where I can sit around and wait for four years and never get my opportunity. Unfortunately, we have a couple of guys who are good players and in the same class, and so it's been difficult in that sense. But last year I got my chance and I felt like I played pretty well. We won the national championship and I was thankful that I was able to really contribute to all that; and that makes it that much more special to me."

"A lot of people," Doleman inserted, "talk about the fact that you've not had the senior season you'd hoped to have. But they talk about you going on and playing in the NFL as somebody who could be a quality backup for several years and then move into a starting position. Do you see that for yourself?"

"I think so," Brook responded without hesitation. "It's definitely one of my dreams and something I've always had as a goal. And I'm going to give it every shot I have. I think I have the ability and I hope I get the opportunity."

"There probably hasn't been a more popular backup quarterback in the whole country," Doleman observed. "I mean the whole state of Nebraska knows who Brook Berringer is. That has to be somewhat enjoyable to go through things like that and have opportunities where people do recognize you and appreciate what you've done."

"Well, it's been great," Brook agreed, "and the fans and the people around the state of Nebraska are just incredible. I've said it a lot of times, but it's just unbelievable to me to come up into this situation and play for the Big Red, and experience what it's really like to have these kind of fans and this kind of tradition. No matter where I go the fans are always true and they're very genuine. It's a neat thing and it makes me appreciate being part of this kind of program."

"Do you look back," Doleman asked, "and have any regrets, thinking you should have done it any differently?"

"Well, it has been tough," Brook admitted, "in the sense that I have wanted to start. I've wanted to play more than what I have. But I don't know that I'd do it any differently. I really appreciate all the opportunities I've been given and the playing time I've gotten. And if it all works out in the end, everything will be fine. But there's no substitute for this kind of a program. And even if I'd gone somewhere else and maybe started for two or three years, I don't think I would've have had the kind of experience I've gotten to enjoy here."

Disappointment? Yes!

But Brook is a champion who learned how to ingest the frustrations of life and grow stronger.

Bitterness? No!

Brook wouldn't allow such a negative to lodge in his heart. Rage and anger destroy the bitter one. Most people in this world do not know how to handle hurt and injury: when struck they tend to lash back. But a few, like this man, take the fury of pain and transform it into a balm in order to soothe the anguish of others. The trials Brook endured throughout the 1995 season caused his faith to grow steadily. And his maturing faith was apparent to many of those around him.

"There comes a point in every person's life where your faith has to be transferred from that of your family and your parents to what your faith really is," Tom Osborne explained several months after Brook's death. "And I could sense in the last year that I knew him that Brook had made some decisions along those lines where he himself had become a very committed Christian and was actively working at becoming as strong in his Christian faith as he could be."

CHAPTER 11

BROOK BERRINGER DAY

Certainly his senior season had not gone as he had envisioned or hoped, but Brook was enthusiastic about everything happening in his life. He was confident of his ability, classes were going well, the various hunting seasons were ready to open, and he was continuing to grow in his faith. In a casual opportunity in the weight room, Ron Brown, brought up the subject of Jesus Christ with Brook. Ron already knew about Brook's recent commitment to Christ, and Brook knew that he knew; but they had a good time pretending with each other that it was news.

A few days later, Brook went to Turner Gill's office. He had great respect for his quarterback coach and wanted to share the fact with him directly. "Coach," he said in his quiet way, "I think you already know this, but I wanted you to hear it from me. Several weeks ago I gave my life to Jesus Christ."

"That's great," Turner exulted as he stood to shake Brook's hand. "Yes, I knew, but, man, it thrills me to hear it from you."

Brook was excited about the upcoming game on Saturday against Washington State because it was to be his senior recognition; Brook Berringer Day. His mother had made arrangements to celebrate Brook's special day at Roger Plooster's pond after the game. They planned to roast a pig and serve a variety of wild game. Brook and Jan together invited about 150 friends and relatives to attend, including an entire busload from Goodland and family from the Sutton and Hastings areas.

Brook was already notorious for scrambling to get enough tickets to both home and away games for his family and friends.

"Just see what you can do, please. My uncle (or his cousin, or his friend, or his neighbor, or his . . .) is coming in and I'd really like to help them out," he would plead. It was just like Brook. He was always trying to just "help somebody out."

This time, however, Brook was in the ticket-pinch of his life, needing not just dozens but hundreds of tickets. Family, friends and friends of friends were planning on making the trek to Lincoln for Brook's big day, and he did not want to let them down. With the help of a variety of friends, businesses, the loyal ticket office staff and people he didn't even know, Brook managed to get tickets for almost everyone who had made a request.

As we wrapped up our Thursday meeting that week of the Washington State game, I was thinking about the many conversations we had had about the NFL and Brook's legitimate shot at being drafted. With that in mind, I asked him, "Brook, what do you really want?"

He looked at me across the corner of the table and asked, "What do you mean?"

"You know," I said evasively, not wanting to pin him down to any particulars, "what do you want to see happen in the next four or five years?"

He stared at me steadily for a moment. "Art," he said evenly, "all I really want is to grow in my relationship with Jesus Christ. This is the greatest thing that ever happened to me."

His answer caught me by surprise. While he was thinking about eternal things, my mind was focused on his career. Brook's perspective was changing, and it was exciting to witness it first hand.

Brook was really pumped as he trotted out on the field half-an-hour before game time with the other quarterbacks and the receivers to begin his pregame regimen. It was always the same; loosen his throwing arm up by tossing the ball, then timing patterns with receivers running routes, calisthenics, crisscross leg stepping, stretching exercises with a partner, and finally running mock plays.

He and Matt Turman had talked late the night before about the game and what it meant to Brook. Knowing there would be more of his personal fans, family, and friends at the game than normal; and since he had played so well against Pacific the week before; Brook thought he might be called on early in the Washington State game. To be sure, he was a team player; and the object of any game is to win. But playing time was important to him, as to any true competitor. And he had proven his ability over and over again.

Confidently that afternoon he roamed the sidelines, in step with Coach Gill, through the first quarter. As always, they charted every play so that he knew what Washington State's defense was doing, for when he was called on to play. Again, however, he watched the game through the drizzle for most of the second quarter.

When Brook entered the game, he ran an option play. When he kept the ball, he felt something pop in his knee. But he shook it off as a minor pain; he had known worse.

Once again on the sidelines for all of the third quarter and the start of the fourth, he flexed his leg a dozen times trying to work out the growing soreness. When he was inserted into the game a second time, he carried the ball for a short gain but drew up lame. He had to give way to his friend, Matt.

As had become his custom at the conclusion of every game, Brook gathered with members of the team and players from the opposition in the center of the field for a postgame prayer. This time he stood instead of kneeling. The throbbing pain in his right knee was becoming intense. With an inner concern, he walked toward the dressing room, but made a right turn to the training room. In the next 45 minutes, several syringes of liquid were drawn from his knee where a bursa sac had ruptured.

When Brook's familiar figure finally emerged from the south stadium door more than an hour after the game, dozens of young fans were still hanging around for autographs and scrambled to get to him. Though walking stiff-legged, he paused to sign everything held out to him, determined never to disappoint anyone, never to ignore even a stranger.

He was genuinely relieved when he was able to ease into the

solitude of the front seat of his truck for the short drive home. What had been a bright hope for him five hours before when he arrived at Memorial Stadium had turned as gray and dismal as the Nebraska skies. He had never been in better shape physically and had expected to make a major contribution against a tough opponent. Now, however, he was deeply disappointed. There wasn't an opportunity for him to play much, and he believed he might have to face a tough rehabilitation.

When he got home to change clothes and drive out to the celebration near Malcolm, his knee was already swollen to double its normal size. It took him twice as long to do everything.

Meanwhile, an excited crowd of over 400 people gathered on the shore of the small lake just below Plooster's magnificent country home, unaware that Brook was injured. Dozens of kids carried footballs, most of whom were wearing football jerseys emblazoned with the name "Berringer" and invariably numbered "18." While they waited for a gigantic smoker to finish cooking hundreds of pounds of meat, guests took advantage of cold drinks from several coolers and talked a whole range of subjects while waiting for the guest of honor to arrive.

When at last Brook did arrive and people caught sight of him at the far end of the meadow, the whole scene of activity shifted toward him. Because of the pain in his leg, he did decline the invitation of several youngsters to play football with them; but stooped to lift three or four little ones up in his arms.

It took him nearly two hours to move 60 yards from where the first fans intercepted him to be near the serving lines. He signed his name several hundred times—on programs, footballs, shirts, and caps.

After hours of stories, laughter and food, things began to wind down at the Plooster's lake-front home. The swan that had been swimming back and forth all evening looked for a place to nestle down for the night, and a bonfire lit by the water's edge illuminated the area It had been a big day for Brook. Nearly three times as many people than were invited showed up for the evening event. But while Brook truly appreciated everyone's enthusiasm and support that night and throughout his career at Nebraska, his lack of playing time and injury that day seemed to put a damper on his spirit.

After the crowd had dwindled down to just 30 or 40, most of which were family members, Brook slowly limped toward the bonfire. He thought about his most recent memory verse and tried to find encouragement in it:

> "And we know that in all things God works for the good of those who love him, who have been called according to his purpose."

As he settled down near the fire, Brook decided he had to trust God even when things didn't seem to make sense. Although he felt the pain of his injury and had no idea how God could possibly use it in his life, Brook trusted that God was in control.

Little did he know that it was his perseverance through this and other trials that would help mold a man that God could use to impact those around him in ways he never would have dreamed possible.

CHAPTER *12*

NEVER A DULL MOMENT

No matter what else might come his way, one thing Brook Berringer always had in ample supply was fun. He enjoyed a wide variety of activities. Football, though important, was not the center of his universe. Because he had so many interests, he was in a constant state of motion.

Growing up, he was very sure of what he could do in a physical sense, and he did it. Even at the tender age of three, after seeing the neighbor boy, Scott, ride his bike without training wheels, Brook was ready to get rid of his training wheels as well.

"What are you doing, Brook?" asked his mother, as Brook tore through the house obviously looking for something.

"Where are dad's tools?" he asked.

"Why do you need your dad's tools?" Jan asked.

"I want to take my training wheels off my bike. The boy across the street doesn't have them on his bike" he insisted.

"But Brook, he's six years old. He doesn't need training wheels. When you're six, you won't need them either," Jan offered, hoping to thwart his mission.

"I don't care. I can ride my bike without them," Brook stated.

"Well, your dad will be home Friday afternoon. You'll have to wait until then so he can take the training wheels off for you," Jan said sternly.

On Friday afternoon, Brook sat at the end of the driveway next to his bike with pliers and screwdriver in hand, waiting for his dad.

When Warren arrived home from a week of radiation treatments in Colorado Springs, he had no more than opened his car door when Brook asked him to please take off his training wheels. His father obliged, and that afternoon, Brook rode his bike up and down the street with pride–and without training wheels.

Nevertheless, he wasn't so bold and daring in everything. When it came to interpersonal relationships, he generally was reluctant to invade the space of anyone, or to make the first approach. It was a gentle show of shyness, which in time worked to his advantage. In his quiet attitude, he took time to observe other people closely, developing a keen judgment of personality to the point that it was difficult for someone to delude him with words. He believed that the true test of a person is what affect his or her actions have on others. So he watched.

As he did, he developed a high standard for himself, a goal of looking out for the needs of others. Having been hurt himself, and being so conscious of how deep pain can go, he never wanted to bring hurt to anyone. On the contrary, he wanted to help everyone he met to see the brighter side of life. That's one reason he would decide, on the spur of the moment, to go visit in a hospital ward– sometimes bringing other football players with him.

But even then, he didn't give long speeches to draw attention to himself. His glowing smile and a firm handshake were his primary tools of communication. Brook was not the type of man who belabored a subject with words; he never wasted any. It was the thought or feeling or actions behind what someone said that mattered to him–and that's how he interacted with others.

If sportswriters had understood that, especially during the year he was in the spotlight, they would have hit a gold mine. But they were always on a deadline, always in a hurry. It takes time to listen to what a person isn't saying. By and large the pundits asked him cliché questions and missed the richness of the man himself. What he really thought about significant matters seldom got into print.

Sadly one writer lamented, "Babbling Brook, he's not."

True. Deep waters run still. But they last and they are mighty.

Those few who took the time found someone far more significant than a quick story about a quarterback, who oddly enough was a sportsman of many facets—hunter, fisherman, pilot.

Far below the cool exterior which Brook exuded, was a man of infinite proportions: compassionate, intelligent, and full of fun. Here was a man's man.

Why did Brook have such a zest for life? He literally ran through it, leaving friends and associates breathless in trying to maintain the pace. And yet he had the energy to do it all well. Was God, by His grace, enabling this young man to cram his "three-score-years-and-ten" into less than a quarter of a century?

One thing that those close to Brook knew and appreciated about him was his keen wit which could please you with his "one liners," or snare you with his practical jokes.

His hunting partner and house mate, Brad Wells, was the prize object of one of Brook's favorite tricks of all time. He planned it one Sunday afternoon around Halloween of 1995, and everything fell perfectly into place far beyond what he had imagined.

Brad was out all day hunting with friend, Tom Rush. While they were gone, Brook stuffed a pair of blue jeans with newspapers and laid them out at the side of Brad's bed, then put cowboy boots in place, so that it looked like the lower part of a body. The supposed torso was covered over, giving the appearance of a dead body.

Weary from a long day of hunting, Brad and Tom pulled in around 11:00 p.m. As they walked up to the house, Brad saw Brook come out the side door and was relieved that someone had been there that evening. Their neighborhood seemed to have its share of transients and Brad always liked to come home knowing someone had been around all day. As they got inside, they headed for Brad's room to dump off some of their gear. Tom stopped immediately after the light when on. Brad impatiently looked past him and saw the legs sticking out from under his comforter on the floor.

"My first reaction was that it was a dead guy," Brad later said.

The two "moon-walked" out of the room and headed outside. Brook was there with the dogs as Brad and Tom approached him about the visitor.

"So, who's that in my room?" Brad quizzed Brook.

"What do you mean? I've been here all night and I didn't see anyone," Brook replied with a completely straight face.

Then, just as Brad went to point out the mystery man through his window, his dog happened to leave the bedroom at the same time and bumped the bedroom door on the way out. This perfectly timed, but coincidental movement, gave Brad the impression that the man was now wandering around the house.

As Brad went back inside, Brook filled Tom in on the prank. The two laughed hysterically, but vowed to keep it a secret as long as they possibly could. When they went back through the side door to check on Brad's investigation, Brook finally found him on the landing outside their door, with his shotgun in hand.

"What are you doing out here?" Brook demanded.

"I'm not moving until they get here," Brad responded matter-of-factly.

"Who?" Brook asked.

"The police!" Brad said.

"What? What did you say?" Brook pleaded.

"I called 911!" Brad replied.

"You what?!" Brook exclaimed, immediately drained of all humor.

The sound of sirens was all the answer he got as he leaped to his feet.

"Brad! It's a joke!" he exclaimed

Brad looked at his friend in amazement. "Oh, oh," he said.

Brad immediately headed for the door and met the paramedics from the fire truck on the sidewalk. He explained that it was a false alarm and that the body ended up being a dummy. As the police and paramedics slowly left the "scene of the crime" Brook, Brad and Tom could stifle the pain born of laughter no longer and each enjoyed a good hearty laugh at the prank that would go down as one of Brook's greatest.

Surely one of Brook's favorite targets was his quarterback buddy, Matt Turman. In the team locker room at Memorial Stadium, the quarterbacks' section is just inside the door. Two other players' lockers were between Matt and Brook, but Brook didn't bother them with his prize water trick–he saved it just for Matt. Above the bench and an open space for hanging clothes is a double-door cabinet. A cup of water, tilted just right inside the door, could properly drench any unsuspecting victim.

Brook, joined by several other players anticipating the baptism, roared with laughter as the paper cup emptied its contents on Turman.

Matt laughed, too. He could never be angry with Brook whom he admired so much.

Remembering the joy of "getting" Matt the first time, Brook set up his trap a second time, a few weeks later. Same result. Same laughter from Brook and others. And Matt? He laughed, of course, but determined also to be more wary of his friend in the future.

Brook, however, was as innovative with tricks as he was in running the football. The next time he wanted to show Matt how much he loved him, he simply greased the inside of his helmet with Vaseline. Matt thought it slid on too easily. Then, out on the field, after he began to sweat and the goo started running down his forehead, Brook put an arm around his shoulder, and laughed and laughed.

The only retaliation Turman ever tried was to put Icy Hot in Brook's chin strap–which, when it began to work in the heat of the day, really got Brook's attention. As he jerked off the strap, he knew instantly who had done it. From several feet away he caught Matt's eye, and gave him a thumbs up salute for excellence.

Matt laughed, knowing that at some point he would be repaid.

Warren with new son, Brook in the
Scottsbluff hospital – July 1973.

Jan and Brook on July 13,
1973 – the day they came
home from the hospital.

The fishing license Warren
bought Brook four days after
Brook's birth.

1973 RESIDENT FISH

STATE OF NEBRASKA

7-13-73   514-36-5293 105227
DATE   SOCIAL SECURITY NO.

BROOK WARREN BEREINGER
NAME

2075 PRIMROSE AVE,
STREET

SCOTTSBLUFF, NEBRASKA 69361
TOWN   STATE   ZIP

MO. 7 DAY 9 YEAR 73 M 22" 9'10 BRN BLUE
DATE OF BIRTH SEX HT. WT. HAIR EYES

TEMPO SESS
DEALER   EXPIRES DEC. 31, 1973

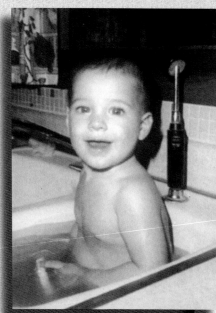

Brook at age six months.

Warren tossing one-year-old Brook into the air – August 1974.

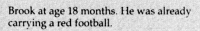

Brook at age 18 months. He was already carrying a red football.

Brook caught his first fish at two years of age at State Lake near Goodland, Kansas.

Brook with his best farming buddy, cousin Kent Willems, at Grandpa Ochsner's farm. Both are 3 years old in the above picture.

Warren and Brook (age three) with a new bicycle. It was an early fourth birthday present.

The night before opening day of pheasant season. Brook and Warren always laid their clothes out ready to dive into them at 5:00 a.m.

Warren with Brook – January 1981.

Six-year-old Brook wearing the leather cowboy outfit his mom made for him – Christmas 1979.

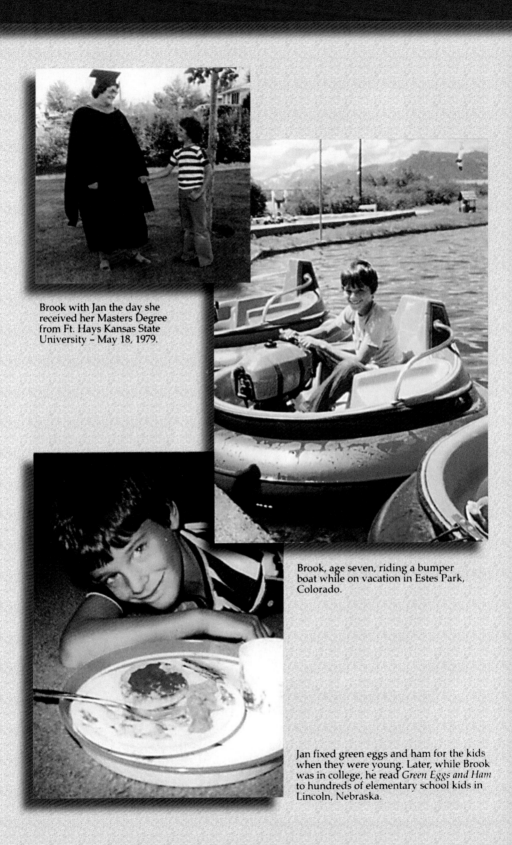

Brook with Jan the day she
received her Masters Degree
from Ft. Hays Kansas State
University – May 18, 1979.

Brook, age seven, riding a bumper
boat while on vacation in Estes Park,
Colorado.

Jan fixed green eggs and ham for the kids
when they were young. Later, while Brook
was in college, he read *Green Eggs and Ham*
to hundreds of elementary school kids in
Lincoln, Nebraska.

November 1981 photo of cousins – Back
row l-r – Terri Workman, Mike McClure,
Mitch McClure, Tony Workman, Robyn
Berringer and Jamie McClure (Mitch's
wife). Front row l-r – Todd Berringer,
Brook, Nicoel, Brett Berringer, and Drue.

Brook with favorite companion,
Freckles.

Brook enjoyed flying early – here
shown riding with cousin Kevin
on an ultralight at Uncle Ken and
Aunt Roma Troutt's ranch in
Idaho in 1981 – Summer 1981.

Christmas at Uncle Stan and Aunt Jolene's in 1981 –
Drue, Jan, Brook, and Nicoel.

Eight-year-old Brook after pheasant hunting
on November 14, 1981.

Nicoel, Drue, and Brook at Disneyland
in the summer of 1982.

Brook during baseball season at age seven.

Brook began playing the trombone in fifth grade.

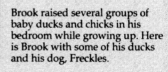

Brook raised several groups of baby ducks and chicks in his bedroom while growing up. Here is Brook with some of his ducks and his dog, Freckles.

Brook would squirt dish soap on the trampoline, set a sprinkler underneath and jump in the mountain of suds.

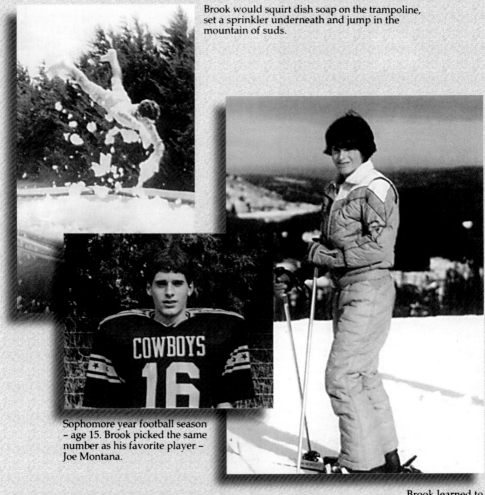

Sophomore year football season – age 15. Brook picked the same number as his favorite player – Joe Montana.

Brook learned to snow ski when he was eight years old

Brook three wheeling with cousin Kent Willems – Fall 1985.

Drue, Nicoel, and Brook at cousin Robyn's wedding in June 1985.

Seventh grade basketball tournament in Scott City, Kansas. (Brook is No. 10).

Aunt Jolene Ellis, Drue, Brook, Nicoel, and Uncle Stan Ellis at "Warren's Meadow" near Estes Park, Colorado, July 25, 1992.

Tiffini Lake, Brook, Nicoel, Drue and Tobey Lake on a ski trip to Copper Mountain, Colorado in the spring of 1993.

Brook skiing.

Brook and Grandpa Berringer after a day of turkey hunting.

Nicoel, Brook and Drue at the Lincoln airport as Brook departs for his first Orange Bowl.

Brook, Jan, Nicoel, Kevin, and Drue on the day of Nicoel and Kevin's wedding, August 13, 1994.

Jan and Brook the evening of Kevin and Nicoel's wedding.

Ellen Brook, Brook's niece, was baptized on August 11, 1996.

Uncle Willie, Nicoel, Aunt Judy, Kevin, Drue, Grandma Ochsner, close friends Jerry and Jeanne McCue, and Jan after the Wyoming game in 1994.

Drue with Brook on the sidelines of Memorial Stadium during the 1994 season.

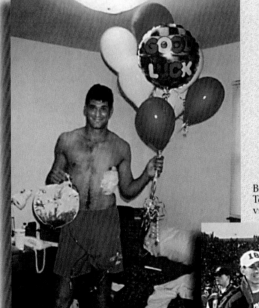

Brett, Uncle Willie, Chris Wilson, Tiffini, Drue, Jan, Todd, Aunt Judy, and Todd's wife Angie after NU vs. OU game, 1994.

Brook holds a bag which is collecting fluid from his punctured lung after the Wyoming game – 1994 season.

Brook with Jan after
a game during the
1994 season.

"Brook and Company" – Family and friends at the 1995 Orange Bowl.

Drue, Nicoel, and Tiffini in Miami at the 1995 Orange Bowl.

Jan, Nicoel, Kevin, Drue, and Brook
on January 1, 1995 – the morning of
the 1995 Orange Bowl.

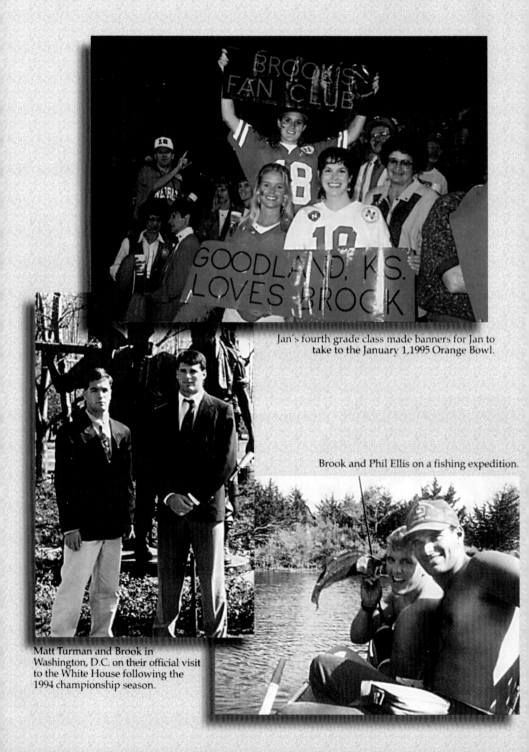

Jan's fourth grade class made banners for Jan to
take to the January 1,1995 Orange Bowl.

Brook and Phil Ellis on a fishing expedition.

Matt Turman and Brook in
Washington, D.C. on their official visit
to the White House following the
1994 championship season.

Brook with Juke and new puppy Bodie (Juke's son).

Brook enjoyed talking to
school assemblies during
his career at Nebraska.
He's shown here speaking
to kids in Malcolm,
Nebraska.

Troy Lake and Brook show their catch
for the day at Moose Lake in Minnesota
– July 1995.

Brook and Tiffini with the Sawyer Brown country western
band – Summer 1995.

Brook and good friend Dr. A.H. Domina.

Bodie, Juke, and Brook after a morning of hunting near Lincoln, Nebraska.

Brad Wells and Brook

Brook and Brad Wells

Brook with close friend and author, Art Lindsay.

Uncle Willie and Brook after a day of turkey hunting.

Brook with a few of his fans at Roger
Plooster's pond on Brook Berringer Day.

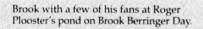

Brook signs
autographs the
evening of Brook
Berringer Day,
September 30, 1995.

Brook and his junior high quarterback mentor, Leo Hayden.

Drue and Brook during fall season of 1995.

Brook and Tiffini after a few hours of pheasant and quail hunting.

Brook and Jan with Aunt Judy Berringer, Marilyn Neef, Laura Saf, Drue, and Aunt Judy McClure.

Uncle Stan, Aunt Jolene, Brook, Drue, Grandma Ochsner, Nicoel, and Jan after the NU vs. KU game 1995.

Brook got this five-point buck in December 1995 on A.B. Fisher's ranch near Brewster, Kansas.

Brad Wells, after being fooled by Brook's "Deadman" prank.

Leo Hayden, Dax Hayden, Seth Hayden, Brook and Uncle J.B. McClure.

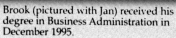

Brook (pictured with Jan) received his
degree in Business Administration in
December 1995.

Brook with former Husker All-American
Trev Alberts, while in Indianapolis for the
NFL Combine in February 1996.

Brook and his close friend, Dev Mull.
Dev played baseball at Fort Hays,
Kansas State University.

Brad Wells, Jim McKee, and Brook after
a day of coyote hunting.

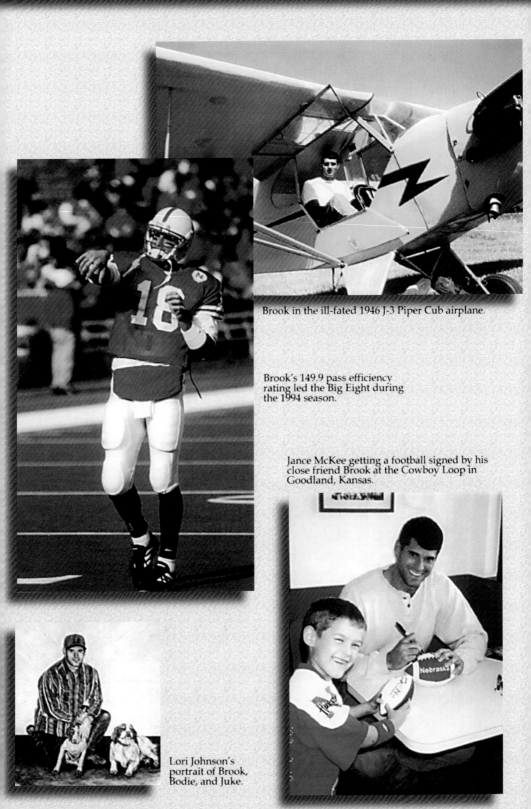

Brook in the ill-fated 1946 J-3 Piper Cub airplane.

Brook's 149.9 pass efficiency rating led the Big Eight during the 1994 season.

Jance McKee getting a football signed by his close friend Brook at the Cowboy Loop in Goodland, Kansas.

Lori Johnson's portrait of Brook, Bodie, and Juke.

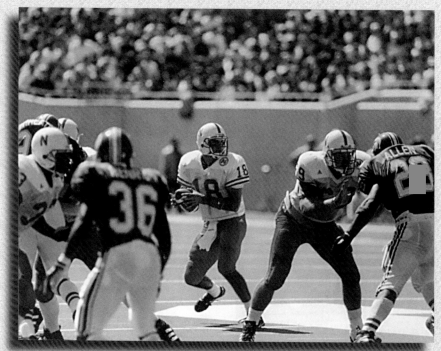

Brook helped lead his team to a 50-10 victory over Michigan State in September 1995. During this game he threw a 51-yard toss to Reggie Baul.

Brook was 10 for 15 for 75 yards passing during the first half of the 1994 Oklahoma State game. Brook sat out the second half as X-rays taken at halftime showed his lung had partially collapsed.

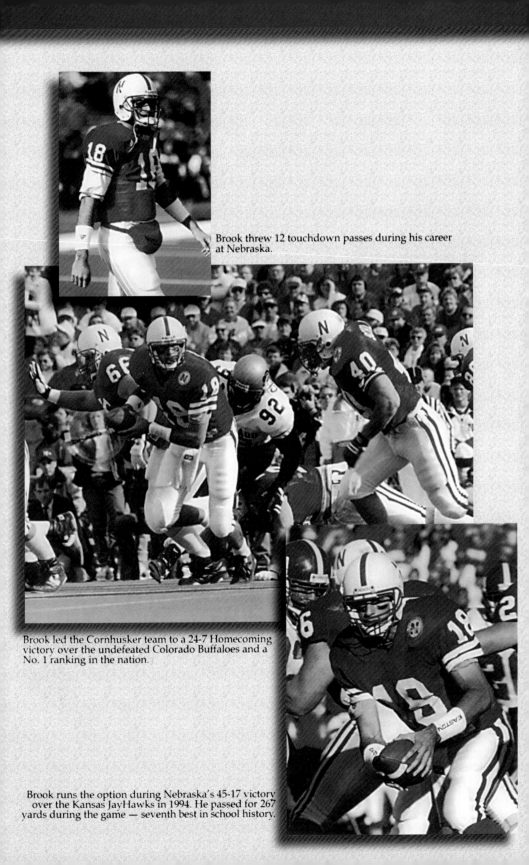

Brook threw 12 touchdown passes during his career at Nebraska.

Brook led the Cornhusker team to a 24-7 Homecoming victory over the undefeated Colorado Buffaloes and a No. 1 ranking in the nation.

Brook runs the option during Nebraska's 45-17 victory over the Kansas JayHawks in 1994. He passed for 267 yards during the game — seventh best in school history.

Brook led the Big Eight in completion
percentage during the 1994 season at
63.2%. This was the best completion rate
during the Big Eight schedule for a
Nebraska quarterback in 20 years.

Brook ended the 1994 regular season
with his seventh start and seventh
victory – a 13-3 win over the Oklahoma
Sooners in Norman. He was also named
ABC Sports' Most Valuable Player after
the nationally televised game.

Brook helped lead his team to a 24-17
victory, and a national championship,
against the Miami Hurricanes on
January 1, 1995.

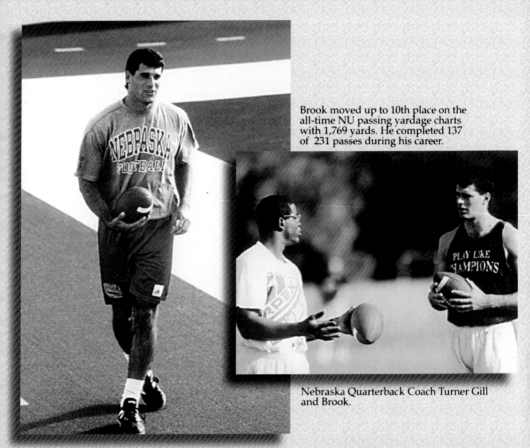

Brook moved up to 10th place on the all-time NU passing yardage charts with 1,769 yards. He completed 137 of 231 passes during his career.

Nebraska Quarterback Coach Turner Gill and Brook.

Brook and teammates praying with Coach Ron Brown and Florida players after the 1996 Fiesta Bowl.

Brook and Coach Tom Osborne with their Big Eight Championship, Orange Bowl, Fiesta Bowl and National Championship trophies.

The "Influence" portrait was passed out to each player speaking at the Fellowship of Christian Athletes banquet on April 18, 1996.

Brook, "the best-known back-up quarterback in the country," played in the 1996 Hula Bowl.

JOIN US IN CELEBRATING
THE LIFE OF

Brook Warren Berringer

ENTERED THIS LIFE
July 9, 1973   Scottsbluff, Nebraska

DEPARTED THIS LIFE
April 18, 1996   Lancaster County, Nebraska

SERVICE
Max Jones Fieldhouse
Monday   April 22, 1996   11:00am
Pastors Dan Bowman and Loren Strait, officiating
Goodland, Kansas

SPEAKERS
Dr. Tom Osborne, Turner Gill, Art Lindsay, Ron Brown
Stan Ellis, John Palmquist, Marty Melia, Rocky Welton

MUSIC
Owen Freiburger
Janet Redlin
GHS X-Pressos

INTERMENT
Goodland, Kansas Cemetery

CASKETBEARERS

Dax Hayden	Phil Ellis	Mark Miller
Devlin Mull	Brad Wells	Tony Veland
Chris Wilson		Clester Johnson

Mitch McClure	Kent Willems	Tony Workman
Mike McClure	Kyle Willems	Gary Thompson
Todd Berringer	Brett Berringer	Justin Eisenach
	Curt Ellis	

HONORARY CASKETBEARERS

Harry Barr	Alan Domina	A. B. Fisher
Norm Ford	Leo Hayden	Jim McKee
Roger Plooster	Roger Saf	Jeff Schmahl

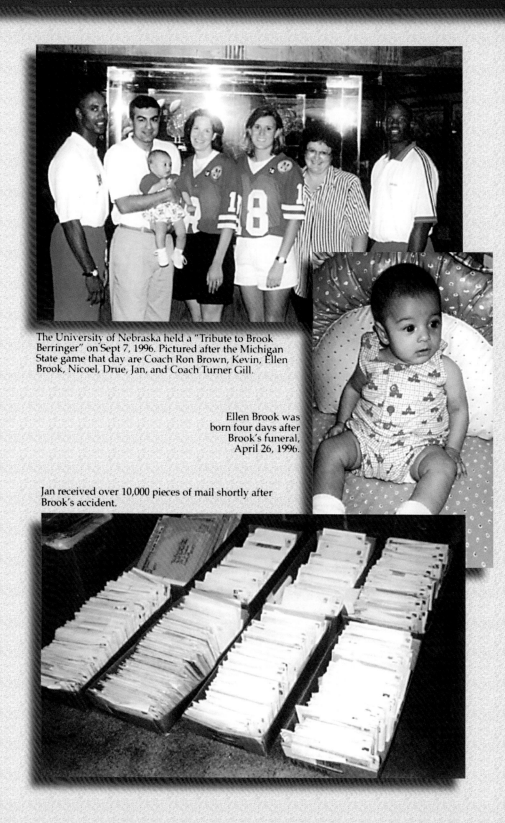

The University of Nebraska held a "Tribute to Brook Berringer" on Sept 7, 1996. Pictured after the Michigan State game that day are Coach Ron Brown, Kevin, Ellen Brook, Nicoel, Drue, Jan, and Coach Turner Gill.

Ellen Brook was born four days after Brook's funeral, April 26, 1996.

Jan received over 10,000 pieces of mail shortly after Brook's accident.

The 1996 Nebraska football team dedicated their season to Brook Berringer by wearing a #18 decal on the back of their helments.

WATCHING FROM THE SIDELINES

U nfortunately, Brook's burst bursa sac injury from the Washington State game was serious. Fortunately, there was an extra week off in the schedule and he had more time to heal before the Missouri game.

Brook hobbled to his classes on Monday and Tuesday, and sat in on the team meetings, determined not to miss out on any part of the game plan for Saturday. Though the weekend had been a setback in his hopes for recovery, he wanted to be prepared. As he confidently told Ken Hambleton of the *Lincoln Journal-Star* in an interview that week, "I'm not going to let any chance pass me by."

However, the trainers were of little help in bringing down the swelling from his knee. By Wednesday, he still couldn't flex it more than an inch or two, and the muscles in his thigh had atrophied to the point that his thigh had shrunk an inch in size. Still, he sat in on the team meetings and huddled with the other quarterbacks and Coach Gill.

Missouri was not expected to be a difficult game for Nebraska. The Tigers were at the bottom of the Big Eight standings. Nevertheless, the Cornhuskers never take any opponent lightly and preparation was total and focused.

The weather at game time on Saturday was dreary, damp, and cold.

Everyone knew that, in spite of the determination of his heart, Brook would not play that day because he couldn't run 10 feet without extreme pain. Nonetheless, when the team came out on the field for the pregame warm up, there in full uniform was Brook. He chatted encouragement to other team members.

It was an agonizing sight then, for everyone in Memorial Stadium to see, when the team trotted off the field to the locker room. Brook could only limp by himself, at the rear of the pack.

Though there was no chance at all that he'd get into the game, Brook marched back and forth along the sidelines with Coach Gill and Matt Turman throughout the first quarter. His desire and drive to be involved, and to contribute to the team made him ignore the pain. He tried to flex his knee occasionally to work the cold out of it, but the stiffness increased steadily. In the second quarter Brook sat down whenever the defense was on the field, but then gamely took up his position once again on the sideline as soon as Nebraska was in control of the ball.

As expected, it was a runaway game. By halftime there was no doubt of the outcome. As the Huskers rushed from the field for the momentary warmth of the locker room, Brook was at the back of the pack once again, unable to run with his teammates. He was pleased with the score but felt disappointed that he'd made no contribution himself.

When the team emerged from under the stands for the second half, Brook had wisely discarded his football uniform and was dressed warmly in sweats and a full-length parka. He didn't pace along the sidelines, but sat with teammates. Outwardly he joked with his friends, but inwardly his heart and mind were in turmoil. More than anything else, he wanted to be out there on the field. Yes, he thought it was nice that Nebraska was winning 57-0. But he was not a football fan–he was a quarterback. And quarterbacks are supposed to play, not watch.

Just him being there, knowing he was in real pain, was encouraging to his teammates, who held him–and his prevailing, positive attitude–in such high respect.

Even with the extra week off in the mid-season schedule, Brook's knee injury mysteriously refused to heal. It was not until after another injury, near the end of the concluding game against

Oklahoma, that team doctors determined why his knee was showing such slow response to therapy. They made the necessary corrections in treatment, and Brook's knee slowly began responding.

After another week, he was well enough to play, and made the trip to Boulder for the big battle against the Colorado Buffaloes. He was excited to be back in shape and to have an opportunity against the same highly-rated team which he had helped to humble the year before. Brook's spirit was as bright as the sunshine during the pregame warm up, and also when he trotted from the locker room for the second half.

Unfortunately, Brook was only needed as a backup. When he entered the game it was all but over in the 44-21 victory. There were only 49 seconds to play as he was sent in for a cameo appearance to handle the final two snaps.

Because the game was being played so close to his hometown, and there were more Berringer fans in the stands than usual, it was disappointing for Brook to play so little. What mattered to him most were his family and close friends. They were a primary focus of his life, and he hated to ever let them down.

Against Iowa State at home the next week, Brook got into the game midway through the third quarter; but by then the game was over with Nebraska leading 52-7. Nonetheless, Brook was thankful for any opportunity that came his way. He felt good about his performance that afternoon as he led touchdown drives on the next two series to build the Cornhuskers' lead to 66-7 by the end of the quarter.

The following Friday, Brook headed to the stadium for the team's departure to Lawrence for the Kansas game. Snow was beginning to swirl around him as he got out of the car and headed for the Training Table area. Rehabilitation on his leg was complete, and Brook was feeling great. And, having missed the Kansas State game, this home state contest was all the more important to him. Before the team loaded up for their trip, Brook was still scrambling to get enough tickets for all his family members.

Once again, Brook's family showed up in droves to show their support at the game. Jan, Nicoel and Kevin, Drue, Grandma Ochsner, along with Tiffini and members of her family were there with Uncle Stan and Aunt Jolene Ellis from Indianapolis, and there were plenty of 18s on caps and sweatshirts in the visitor section of the stadium.

Brook was called on with 11 minutes left in the second quarter, with Frazier experiencing leg cramps, Nebraska leading 14-0. He handed off twice to gain a first down, then carried the ball to pick up five yards. On his fourth play he tried to pass to Phillips out of the pocket, but Phillips was well behind him. As he pumped to throw, a defender hit his arm and the ball rocketed to the ground. A Kansas player fell on it to recover the fumble. Brook knew that, in the confusion of the play, he should have held onto the ball and taken the sack.

That fumble broke a string of 17 consecutive quarters for Nebraska without a turnover.

This was the last time in his college career that Brook got into a ball game before well into the fourth quarter. His faith helped sustain him through all the setbacks and frustrations he was feeling as his football career at Nebraska was coming to an end.

In the Oklahoma game, to conclude the regular season, Brook carried the ball three times in the fourth quarter to pick up 13 yards. He was especially pleased with the longest of those, but he took a terrific hit and came down hard on his back. He seemed none the worse for wear, however, when he arrived an hour later at the Senior Recognition Celebration hosted at the Eleven Club.

After he had greeted several dozen people, he grabbed an empty seat at a table where he continued to sign autographs and answer questions about both the game and the season.

As the evening drew to a close, various coaches spoke on behalf of each player, who then had a chance to respond. Ron Brown was there to speak for Brook, which he did in glowing terms.

Brook, though hesitant to speak intimately to a crowd of so many strangers, singled out one person for praise. "I thank you all for coming," he said, "and I owe a lot to a lot of people. But there is one person more than any other who's always been there for me: my mom. She's always been my greatest fan, and I love her. Thanks, Mom!"

Short, sweet, and poignant. That's Brook. And that definitely was his mom. Brook's words were short but they were long in meaning. It had been Jan's perseverance, her love and her commitment to her children that had helped mold Nicoel, Brook and Drue into the impressive young adults they had each become. And there was no one who appreciated her efforts more than her son, Brook.

Unbelievably, the next day Brook awoke with swelling in his back, obviously from falling so hard on that one play on "the rug" at Memorial Stadium. Shortly, the lump grew until it looked like a basketball attached to his back. Doctor Clare, the team physician, soon surmised that this had to be connected to whatever had caused the continuing inflammation previously in his knee.

After the doctor reviewed and then altered the treatments, the swelling went down and Brook never had another problem with inflammation.

CHAPTER *14*

GRADUATION

Uith football out of the way for a few days, though still black and blue across his back, Brook plunged into wrapping up his academic responsibilities. Two term papers were due on two successive days. The first one was entitled "The Competitive Success in the U. S. Airline Industry." But he really had to labor over the second one, a 2,000 word essay on Microsoft. Just as he finished his last exam, he faced an unexpected trip back home for the funeral of his girlfriend Tiffini's grandmother. Because of his back injury, it was a painful ride for him. Even sitting in class for an hour the morning he left was unbearable. But he looked forward to being with Tiffini and spending a few moments with his mom.

Brook had maintained a hectic schedule for four months, ever since reporting for the fall football camp in early August. There were many demands on his time, and since he never wanted to disappoint anyone, he scheduled himself to a frazzle: from rendering his version of *Green Eggs and Ham* for preschoolers to being Master of Ceremonies for a Ducks Unlimited banquet. It seemed he was always in motion, so much so that his mother wondered, "When do you sleep?"

That was a good question that had no answer. It was not unusual for Brook to still be on the telephone with family and friends at midnight, and be bright and ready for hunting the next morning at five. And besides the various people in his life, he had to take time with his two dogs, Juke and Bodie, to take them to the fields for training. Or run down the street trying to recapture them when they'd try his patience by bolting from their kennel when his back was turned.

But he loved his dogs, especially Juke who had been his companion back and forth from Goodland many times. Before he got his pickup, Juke would sit right beside him like a sentinel on the front seat of the car. After Jan had crammed the car with food and clean laundry, she'd wave goodbye to both of them when they were headed back to Lincoln.

In the midst of his debilitating pace, Brook lost sight of any desire to "walk" through the mid-year commencement exercises, having never been one for much "pomp and circumstance" anyway. He would much rather be in field boots and a camouflage jacket out in the woods than sitting in a stuffy gymnasium choked by a tie.

His mother reasoned with him, "Brook, this is the real reason you went to college–to get your degree. If you don't go through the graduation, you'll always regret that you missed it. "And I will, too."

Jeff Schmahl, Video Production Specialist for the Athletic Department, also added a subtle pressure. He wanted footage of the graduation for a promotional piece he was putting together on Brook for telecast later.

Not too enthused about it at the moment, and just hours before the deadline, Brook relented and got his order in for a cap and gown. Once he made that decision, he became excited about it and looked forward to the occasion. "I can't believe I was even thinking about not going through graduation," he said, "to have it all finalized. It seems like for five years you kinda lose track of the goal once in awhile. But it'll be good to have that degree."

By making that decision only three days before the commencement ceremonies scheduled for December 16, no one was bothered by graduation announcements from Brook. Nor was there a large Berringer contingent on hand as there had been for every one of his football games. His mother and sister Drue drove up the night before from Goodland. And while Tiffini came up from Kansas City, Nicoel and Kevin weren't able to get off work, so they were forced to stay home.

On what otherwise turned out to be an absolutely wonderful day, there was one sorry disappointment. Drue woke up in her motel room that morning with a fever and extremely sick to her stomach with a 24-hour virus. Knowing she would miss Brook's graduation event gave her greater distress than the sickness itself. If ever there was a sister who loved her brother devotedly and without question, it was Drue.

Brook hurriedly knotted his tie, grabbed his cap and gown, and jumped into his pickup truck to head to the Devaney Center for the graduation exercises. Near the complex, traffic was at a standstill. Doing what any graduate late for graduation would do in that situation, Brook drove one side of his truck up onto the sidewalk and proceeded around the vehicles in front of him. Just then a policeman took notice of his move, but before the cop could make his reprimand, Brook held up his graduation cap. Shaking his head, the cop begrudgingly but generously motioned him through.

It was then that the excitement of the event began to grip him. It wasn't like the rush he got in advance of a football game; this was more solemn. This was why he'd come to Lincoln—to get an education. And he'd earned it. Something no one could ever take away from him.

One of the first people he saw in the track complex, where the graduates were assembling, was his good friend Clester Johnson, also a mid-term graduate. "Congratulations, man!" Brook exclaimed as they shook hands. "We made it."

"Yeah, you too," Clester responded

"Hey, Brook," a youngster yelled from 20 feet away. And immediately Brook, readily recognized in a crowd, was surrounded by family and friends of other graduates, wanting his autograph on the red commencement program.

CHAPTER 15

FIESTA BOWL

Brook was enthused about Nebraska being on the verge of gaining a second straight national championship. The camaraderie within the band of 21 seniors added to the excitement of playing in their last game together. Those relationships, especially the consistent words of encouragement from most of his senior teammates kept Brook at the core of the team.

And it worked both ways. Though not on the field much, he was a steady inspiration to others by the way he handled the situation, by reaching out to others–ignoring instead of complaining about his own disappointment. Brook was highly thought of by his fellow teammates. As teammate Mark Gilman put it, "Brook could make a person's day just by asking them how they were doin.' "

Nonetheless, Brook knew that his football world had made a 180-degree turn in 12 months. In that period of time, after being 7-0 as a starter, he had not started a game; and in the current season was all but forgotten by the media–though he was widely sought after by fans wherever he happened to be.

Although his senior season had been disappointing at times, he processed one disappointment after another into a greater determination to achieve at the next level. He survived on a firm belief that God would have the final word as to his worth; therefore there was no bitterness in his resolve. He had an amazing capacity to take whatever came his way, good or bad, in stride.

As he told a group of students in an assembly, "You're going to have these rough spots in your life, and the important thing is to be a finisher. So perseverance is a key in my life, and I think it should be a key in everybody's life.

"The ability to overcome adversity is going to be very important in your life."

As Brook prepared to leave for the Fiesta Bowl, he took some time in the team's meeting room to reflect on the season. He realized that throughout his difficult times, it was the peace he experienced in his new relationship with God that was really helping keep his attitude in check. That was exciting to Brook, and it caused him to look even more forward to the Fiesta Bowl.

Of Brook's final season and the subsequent months following, Coach Osborne was later quoted saying, "The thing that I appreciated about Brook, was when things were going great he was still the same guy–he didn't change. And when things weren't going so great as far as playing time he was still the same guy. He gave it all he had. He was very positive. He had to be somewhat disappointed (with his lack of playing time), but he didn't let it show–he was a great team person."

During the intervening week, Brook had great practice times. His physical problems were behind him. The only thing he had asked of the trainers in Lincoln before leaving was that they have plenty of extra-strength Tylenol on hand. His timing was excellent and he felt well and rested, but he had nagging doubts that he'd see much action in the game. "I haven't had as many snaps in practice as I'd like," he said. "I just hope I get a chance to play."

The Fiesta Bowl was a fabulous occasion for the Cornhuskers. After allowing some early success to a highly touted Florida team, Nebraska took control of the game on both sides of the ball and went into the locker room at halftime with a comfortable 35-10 lead. Brook started warming up on the sideline when four minutes into the third quarter Tommie Frazier got a leg cramp. Standing next to Frazier while a trainer massaged his calf muscle, Brook anticipated getting into the game.

Nebraska and Florida traded possessions without any scoring for the next eight minutes before Frazier broke through on a quarterback draw: 42-10.

Florida struck back quickly and with a two-point conversion made the score 42-18.

Frazier closed out the third quarter with an unbelievable, multiple-tackle-breaking run: 49-18.

After Tony Veland intercepted Florida on its next series of downs, Frazier trotted out onto the field. Then it was three downs-and-out. On the punt, however, Florida fumbled and Nebraska had the ball on the Florida 22-yard line.

Although Brook was disappointed that he hadn't gotten into the game, he applauded along with everyone else as Lawrence Phillips rushed into the end zone: 55-18.

With a little over six minutes to play in the game, after Florida couldn't move the ball, Brook was sent into the game to handle the ball a half-dozen times and carry the ball into the end zone on a quarterback sneak.

Although he wasn't able to play a significant role in the game, Brook was every bit as excited as his teammates about the win. Following the game, he joined his teammates for one last huddle. With Coach Brown between them, Brook and Florida quarterback Danny Wuerffel knelt for prayer in the center of the field, surrounded by several dozen of their teammates.

In the locker room afterward, because his team had dominated Florida so decisively, the atmosphere was not as festive as after the Miami game a year earlier.

Nebraska had a second consecutive national football championship.

Brook's football career as a Cornhusker was at an end.

However, while in Arizona, there were two other things that happened that week which in time would prove to be an invaluable blessing to thousands.

The six-minute video clip, which Jeff Schmahl had so expertly edited for telecast in the Lincoln area the Sunday before the Fiesta Bowl, was viewed by thousands. But after Brook's death on April 18, portions of that presentation have been seen nationally by hundreds of thousand of fans. After what appeared to most people as an untimely tragedy, they wanted to know who this guy was.

In the video, Schmahl does highlight Brook's football talent, crediting him in the 1994 season as being "the key player in the Huskers drive to the 1994 national championship. But in 1995 Brook has gone from hero to merely the best backup quarterback in the country."

Brook responded, "I think it takes a lot of character to go through some of the things I've gone through. It can be very frustrating sitting on the sidelines when you've been there in the starting role and you're watching someone else out there. But I've been supportive; and hopefully, I've been a good leader through the starting role, and in the backup role as well. And I consider that's what's most important for this team. So I haven't had any problem with that mission."

The video then highlights some of Brook's play in the Orange Bowl . . . his touchdown pass; and his awesome 51-yard toss in the Michigan State game early in the season. Schmahl explains, "But a series of injuries and Frazier's superb play has kept Brook out of the spotlight in 1995. Even so, Brook has not become bitter."

"I wouldn't change a thing about my decision to come here," Brook responded. "The things that have happened, I don't have any regrets. You know, I've learned a lot about life; and that's the most important thing. I've learned what it takes to persevere and overcome a lot of adversity. And those are things that are going to help out a lot, later in life. And I think that's a part of what the whole aspect of being a college football player in a big-time program like this is all about."

Schmahl goes on to explain, "Brook Berringer is able to keep a great attitude and perspective because his life is not just about football. He has taken an active role as a team leader and role model to numerous children." As the film shows the big football player in a school setting with hundreds of children, and then his December graduation from Nebraska, Schmahl moves on to point out, "While

Brook plays football, his real passion is hunting, whether it's walking the fields of eastern Nebraska with his two brittany spaniels, or spending a cold morning in a duck blind on the Platte River."

For any lover of nature, the footage of Brook hunting pheasant and his gentle words with his dogs is a moving sight. But his comments at dawn in the duck blind are vintage Berringer, "Ah, this is great," he says. "It's a nice, cold, clear morning. Got some ducks flying already. Hopefully we'll get some to decoy in and get some shooting here in a little while. The sun's just coming up through the trees. It's a beautiful morning."

The time Brook spent hunting and fishing were much more than a sport and relaxation time for him. They were continuing bonding times with his father. "I think about him every day," he concluded. "From the time I lost him and growing up through grade school, through high school, and in college, it hasn't gotten any easier. The pain of missing him has gotten worse. But my dad was a very strong Christian and that's something else that he's instilled in me and it's very important to me. And I feel like he's watching me every step of the way; and I can feel his presence at times. When I step out on that football field I know he's out there watching me. When I'm out there walking through the fields with my bird dogs, I know he's walking there right beside me. So that's the way I feel about it, the way I look at it; and that makes it all the more special for me.

"When I'm out there throwing a touchdown pass, I know that my dad's got the best seat in the house."

A second event, taped by telephone from Tempe, was a radio interview conducted by Ron Brown the Friday before the Fiesta Bowl and heard by a few thousand people on his weekly program, "Husker Sports Report." However, since April 18 it has been rebroadcast and copied countless times; and has been an inspiration to tens of thousands of fans.

"I've been looking forward to this interview for a long time," Ron began. "He's one of my favorite young men. His name is Brook Berringer, the popular quarterback for the Huskers' football team, who has enjoyed a great deal of notoriety as the guy who helped us win the national championship last year after Tommie Frazier went down with an injury. Many of you have heard of him.

"Brook, it has been a great run. You know, you've gone through so many ups and downs. You've had to go through the down times of not playing a lot early in your career–sometimes it looked like maybe just pie in the sky. Then, all of a sudden, the so called rags-to-riches story. You emerge into the national spotlight as the starting quarterback and help lead us to the national championship, an outstanding season.

"But you had something even greater that took place. I'm sure the greatest 'up' in your life. Why don't you tell us about that, which took place very recently?"

"Okay," Brook agreed. "Well, Art Lindsay, who's a friend of mine and a friend of yours, began sending me some letters that you gave me. Just a lot of prayer. He was praying for me every day. And it was inspiring: I hadn't even met the guy.

"Finally I was able to meet with Art.

"We started meeting together and having some fellowship. And through him, together, I accepted the Lord as my Savior. It was an incredible thing for me. It was something I had really thought a lot about through the last four years of college. I've had a lot of positive influence through Coach Brown and Coach Osborne; and it was something that was really weighing pretty heavily on my mind.

"Through Art, and through the fellowship we had, we sat down together and I just gave my life to the Lord and accepted Him as my Savior.

"It was an incredible thing. Like I said, it was something weighing heavily on my mind. And when I did it, I felt just a great relief; and a lot of things were lifted off my shoulders."

"That's so exciting, Brook," Ron interjected, "because I know myself, Coach Gill, and Art have been praying for you for a number of years now.

"And I just have to say for all those out there listening that the power of a man praying is incredible. Art Lindsay just had a passion for Brook Berringer. He kept writing letters. And what power God can give to just one person to share the Good News with someone else; and, of course, the result is a life saved like Brook Berringer.

"Brook, again more ups and downs this year. And yet your faith, I believe, has helped sustain you through the time. Would you agree?"

"Yeah," Brook replied, "through my whole career I've been on both ends of the spectrum. I've enjoyed the starting position and I've had to suffer through the frustrations of not getting to play at all. And through this whole ordeal I've been able to use my faith as something that is just a complete comfort. It just takes away a lot of those feelings, because when I have something more specific to focus on, like eternal life and my faith in Christianity and my yearning just to grow in that faith it brings everything, the whole scheme of things into focus better. It's just amazing the difference that it's made in my life.

"I know where I'm headed. I know the ultimate goal and it brings everything into perspective. And it makes football, although it is a big part of my life, something that is not as important as maybe I once thought. It really prioritizes things in my life."

"Well, Brook," Ron concluded, "I just want to say this, Buddy, you've been a great inspiration for so many. And everybody is a starting player on God's team; and you certainly are that."

CHAPTER 16

THE HULA BOWL & THE NFL

ven though in the eyes of some, Brook had a ho-hum 1995 football season, pro scouts in the National Football League kept a watchful interest in him, especially his passing arm. He could catapult a pigskin more than half a football field with ease. Scouts had seen what he accomplished and was able to do in leading Nebraska to the national championship in 1994; and they had not forgotten him. Consequently, in November he received an invitation to participate in the postseason Hula Bowl in Honolulu, January 21, 1996.

Following the Fiesta Bowl, Brook began to take focus on what he hoped would be his career for the next several years in the NFL. He had no illusions as to what his chances were. Certainly the statistics of his senior season were of no value in boosting his image with the pros. Therefore, the tests that would be taken in conjunction with the Hula Bowl would be a first crucial step in the process.

The schedule during the week of the Hula Bowl was very precise–which would have been all right if there hadn't been so many snafus. The primary emphasis of the week's schedule was testing by the pro scouts, both physical and psychological. One written exam took nearly four hours, then there were multiple pages of personal background information to be filled out for each one of the teams in the league. Players were also carted around the island for appearances at hospitals and schools. Only minimal attention was given to preparation for the football game itself to be played on Sunday. Brook caught on to this fact early in the week and, rolling with the tide, focused on the testing.

Recognizing that his playing time could potentially be quite minimal, Brook decided to take snaps from center for the place-kicker. He was perfect on his placements during practices.

"I've done it for a long time," he explained. "I figure the more I make myself available, the better chance I have to play."

It was a good plan. Brook knew that with the small amount of exposure he received while standing on the sidelines during the season, he needed to grab any opportunity he could to give the scouts a clear picture of his abilities.

With the hectic schedule the bowl organizers had Brook on, he didn't see much of Hawaii himself. He and some other players rented a car one afternoon to go up to the North Shore; then he got in about 10 minutes of snorkeling on Saturday afternoon before his family got together for dinner at his hotel. That turned out to be a wonderfully relaxed time on the verandah of the restaurant as everyone enjoyed stuffing themselves at the five-table buffet extravaganza. Conversation flowed freely around the table with Brook and Tiffini, her brother Troy, his Uncle Willie and Aunt Judy, Jan, Drue, myself and his teammate/roommate for the week, Phil Ellis.

While Brook had enjoyed his time in Hawaii up to that point, he was still concerned with performing well in the next day's game. He knew the most important part of the week was the testing and interviews with the pro scouts. But he would feel a lot better about his status if he could perform well on the field. He recognized that playing to his potential would probably not be possible when two or three guys would ask him what they were supposed to do everytime they broke from huddle. Without much offensive practice time and so much confusion on the field, Brook knew he would have to just trust that doing his best would have to be good enough.

Brilliant sunshine drenched Aloha Stadium the next afternoon. It was plain hot. Brook felt the offense's lack of practice time would give the defense the advantage in the game. Unfortunately, Brook's prediction of the game was true. Defenders for both the East and West teams had little difficulty in shutting down the opposing offenses. Brook was one of three quarterbacks on the East team, with the basic game plan being that each man would be in for 12 snaps in the first half. The coach (an ESPN color commentator) would then rotate them in the second half.

It was a good thing Brook had made himself available as a holder for the placekicker, or he wouldn't have gotten into the second half at all. On the sidelines, he warmed up three times in anticipation of being inserted in the game, only to sit down again.

The plays that Brook engineered in the second quarter of that game, unknown to anyone at the time except God, were his last.

One topic which frequently came up during discussions was Brook's future in the National Football League. Few Cornhusker fans had any doubt about his ability nor of his determination to achieve his ultimate potential. Those two factors combined always spelled success. Of course that was the pattern he gave to everything. Always involved in many activities, often all at the same time, he threw himself wholeheartedly into them all. Yet the desire to prove himself in football became a primary focus.

It was a cold February morning when Brook left his house at 7:00 a.m. for his flight to Indianapolis for two days of testing and trials at the NFL Combine. Coaches and scouts from all the professional teams would be there to take a closer look at the prospects. Brook enjoyed the Combine, spending a great deal of time with his Aunt Jolene and Uncle Stan from Indianapolis. He also met up with former teammate and current Indianapolis Colt player Trev Alberts.

It was no surprise to his coaches back in Lincoln when Brook turned in the best times of all the prospective quarterbacks tested at the Combine. Brook was encouraged with his performance at the Combine, and he was looking forward to hearing from a few of the NFL teams.

Any enthusiasm that Brook brought home from the Combine, though, was quickly and painfully thwarted. Over the last few months, he had been in and out of the vet's office with his dog, Juke, because of a back injury which continued to deteriorate. When Brook arrived home from Indianapolis, he tried to call his hunting partner from his kennel, but there was no response. After a few moments, Juke crawled out to Brook, dragging his hind legs.

"I'm afraid the vertebrae in Juke's spine have deteriorated to a point where medication or surgery just won't help. Brook, it really would be best for him to have him put down." The veterinarian's words haunted Brook the remainder of the day. He wondered if Juke's climbing and jumping over their eight-foot fence back home had caused the damage to the dog's spine.

Brook called his mom, and the two discussed the few options he had. After crying together for 45 minutes on the phone, Brook faced the reality of what needed to be done.

Back at the clinic, Brook sat talking to Juke, with his loyal companion's head on his lap. Brook reminisced with the dog, reliving their many hunting trips and the wonderful times they had experienced together in the wide open fields of Kansas and Nebraska. When Brook was ready, he motioned for the vet to come into the room to administer the shot. As the needle was drawn Brook sadly said goodbye to his faithful companion.

Tenderly, he took Juke's body out to a hill overlooking the lake where Brook Berringer Day was held, and where they had hunted many birds together. The ground was frozen solid, so he went back to Lincoln, picked up his roommate and hunting partner, Brad, and the two spent four hours digging a decent burial hole.

As they finished, Brook talked to his father, telling him, "Dad, here is the best hunting dog I've ever known. I'm not nearly as sad, knowing that the two of you are together."

A few weeks later, on March 19, NFL coaches and scouts came to Lincoln to test some of the Cornhusker prospects for other positions and to watch Brook throw the ball. No one who had been around him ever doubted that he had an "NFL arm." That afternoon, not only was he almost flawless in hitting the routing patterns of several receivers, his long arm was perfect with pinpoint accuracy to the end zone.

Two weeks after that, on Friday, March 29, Brook took his final passing tests. Quarterback coaches from the Washington Redskins and the Jacksonville Jaguars were supposed to be there, but travel plans had gone awry for the Washington coach. Brook threw several dozen passes to Clester Johnson. Finally the Jaguar coach said, "Let me see your long arm. Can you hit him in the end zone from the 50?"

"Sure," Brook responded. With precision, he took the simulated snap at the 45, faded back to the 50, and hit the streaking Johnson in the end zone.

"How far can you throw it?" the Jaguar coach asked with appreciation in his voice.

"How far do you want me to throw it?" Brook asked with confidence.

"Can you try it from the 40?" the coach suggested.

Without a word Brook nodded. Then, with precision he heaved the ball 65 yards in the air into the waiting arms of a man who had long been one of his favorite targets.

The coach didn't need to see anything else.

NATIONWIDE DEMAND

In the *1995 Nebraska Football Media and Recruiting Guide,* Brook was described as: "One of the Huskers' most active community leaders, he has been a volunteer speaker at several area hospitals, participated in the "School is Cool Jam," Ventures in Partnership, the SCIP Drug Prevention Program and National Education Week, to name a few." That was published well in advance of the 1995 season and listed only those engagements which went through the athletic department.

Of course Brook gained national prominence as a result of his contribution to the 1994 national championship and was readily recognized throughout Nebraska by anyone who knew anything at all about football. The usual question people would ask after thanking him for speaking at their school or function was, "When can you come back?" He did an admirable job of keeping up with the requests for his time, though there was no way he could possibly accommodate them all.

A second thing which put him under extreme scrutiny, and consequent demand, was the manner in which he handled his demotion to second string in the Orange Bowl. That alone endeared him to many thousands of people, who could easily identify with the disappointment he felt. They too had experienced setbacks of one kind or another and empathized with him. What truly captivated them, however, was the poise by which he dealt with the situation–without resentment. Anyone can be a champion at the top. It takes something special to stand tall in decline.

One would think that with Brook on the bench for most of October, November, and December of 1995, with very few printed stories and no television interviews of note (sound bites are precious and reserved for real highlights) that the public would have forgotten about him. After all, it seemed that football had forsaken him. However, just the opposite was true. He had more requests for speaking engagements and other affairs than he could keep up with. He stretched himself to the limit. One type of invitation he never refused, if at all possible, was to share with elementary school children in the Lincoln area. Whenever he was getting ready for one of those opportunities he would jokingly say, "I'm off to another *Green Eggs and Ham* appearance," in reference to the Dr. Seuss story he often read to the children.

After his career at Nebraska ended, his travel schedule took on a national scope, stretching as far as Albuquerque, New Mexico, to be on hand to honor a longtime Cornhusker football booster at a banquet. Fly out, speak, fly back.

He also covered the state of Nebraska, making nearly 50 appearances in the first four months of 1996.

For one of those, on April 2, he traveled to North Platte in the western part of the state where an estimated 3,000 students from 50 different schools gathered for the first ever "School is Cool Jam" in that area. Brook, who received the longest and loudest ovation of any of the athletes on the program, said that the event, for the first time held outside of Lincoln, was long overdue. "We realize that the University of Nebraska doesn't always reach this far out west," he said. "We hope the event continues to get bigger."

After watching several Mid-Plains, St. Pat's and North Platte High School players participate in a basketball dunking contest, Nebraska volleyball standout Allison Weston, who also was on the program, encouraged Brook to try a dunk, too.

Brook never needed much urging to try any challenge. So, cheered on by the students, he borrowed a pair of size 13 tennis shoes from one of the high school seniors. He dribbled the ball back-and-forth at the top of the key; then turning toward the basket, he spun through the air and slammed the ball impressively through the net. The students went wild in their applause, and Brook waved a victory sign with both arms extended high in the air.

What turned out to be his final public appearance, oddly enough, was in his birth hometown of Scottsbluff, Nebraska. Actually it was a misreading of the calendar that got him there. When he accepted the invitation, he thought that the turkey season opened in Nebraska that same weekend and he'd be able to get some hunting in at the same time. As it turned out, the season didn't open until a week later. Therefore, Brook flew up for the occasion from his home in Goodland.

The promotional event on Saturday, April 13, was held at the Nothin' But Nebraska store. This business, like other stores across the state, marketed everything imaginable that devoted Cornhusker fans could possibly want to buy to identify with the Big Red.

Knowledgeable fans coming into the store asked a variety of questions during Brook's brief appearance. Of course, uppermost in everyone's mind was the NFL draft which was only a week away. What did he see as his chances?

"I think the NFL is obviously looking for someone who has a lot of ability," he answered. "But they also want a good leader who is going to be a good person in the community. Hopefully, that's me."

He went on to explain that the pro scouts and coaches were impressed with his times, the best of any quarterback in the current draft: 1.58 in the 10-yard dash, 4.63 in the 40, and a 34.5 inch vertical jump. Also, in the passing tests he had showed the kind of arm strength that made him a top prospect.

"It'll be nice," he admitted, "to be out in the real world and make some money. Hopefully, I'll get that opportunity." In saying so he didn't sound cocky or shy, just a classy response to a good question.

People also asked about the 1994 season. One man in particular brought a full smile of appreciation to Brook's face when he said, "I want to personally thank you for bringing the national championship to Nebraska last year."

"I had some help," Brook chuckled. "But thanks. I never did

doubt my ability. I was just happy to have the chance to prove that to people."

Excitement was also building, even in far off Scottsbluff, for the ring ceremony and the unveiling of Nebraska's second straight national championship trophy the following Friday night in Lincoln. Many who came by the store intended to make the trip across state for the event, and the spring game the next afternoon.

"That's something you dream of," he responded. "Receiving one championship ring last year was great. I never thought about getting two of them, back to back. That's really something."

Typical of the youth who came by Nothin' But Nebraska that evening were a couple of high school girls who stopped in front of his table to get his autograph. Smiles spread across their faces as they stared down at him adoringly. He had a way, even though autograph lines in front of him sometimes were composed of hundreds of people, to make the ones he was dealing with at the moment feel they were special to him—and they were.

It was getting late when Brook finally got up from the table to leave. "Hey, maybe I'll get paid overtime for staying so long," he joked.

His remark brought approving smiles from everyone in the store as they bid him goodbye.

In Goodland, however, his mother wasn't smiling. She was concerned. Heavy storms were rolling off the Rockies in Colorado and the skies were looking ominous. She knew that almost nothing would stop Brook from trying to fly back home that evening—and she hadn't heard from him.

For some reason she always worried when he was flying, but she never harangued him about it. He so loved to fly. It was fast. And he was always in the fast lane.

She was startled when the telephone rang. "Mom," the familiar voice declared. "we're taking off right away. I'll be home in a little over an hour. So don't worry."

Of course she worried.

It was one of the longest hours of her life until she heard him walk in the door.

CHAPTER 18

SENIOR BASKETBALL

One post-career series of events that Brook enjoyed more than any other, were the charity fund-raiser basketball games played by the 21 seniors from the football team. Steve Ott, close friend and former roommate of Brook, a first-team offensive guard, was the primary organizer of the events which covered most of Nebraska and beyond. Enthusiastic crowds greeted the Cornhuskers in their friendly competition against local teams composed generally of area coaches.

The natural athletic ability of the football players was obvious, and there was a certain "Harlem Globetrotters" atmosphere to the evenings. Fun, not winning, was the only goal of every game. Crazy shots and goofy protests against the referees were common; but what brought the loudest cheers was whenever one of their admired Cornhuskers had a successful dunk. Brook's most enjoyable night in that respect was when he came back from a basketball night in northern Nebraska having made 19 dunks.

Another standard feature of a night's entertainment came when there was a foul shot to be made. The player would pick someone out of the audience to do the honors. One night in Beatrice, Nebraska, Brook went up into the stands to get a boy, six or seven years of age, to shoot for him.

When they got out to the foul line, the boy looked up at Brook and commanded, "Hold these," as he held out his hand. Brook stooped over and held out his palm. A smile of surprise swept across his face when the kid dumped six M & M candies in his hand. The stands erupted in appreciative laughter, then applause, as the little boy deftly heaved the ball through the hoop and ran off into the stands. Brook hurried right after him to give back the candies, and coincidentally delighted the crowd by eating one himself.

Later, when hundreds of fans lined up to get autographs, Brook looked across the table at the little boy. Recognizing him immediately, he asked, "Did you eat your candy?"

"Nope," he replied.

"Why not?" Brook asked in surprise.

"Gonna frame 'em," he answered seriously.

Brook looked at him, a bit stunned by the comment, but said nothing as he signed his name.

Amazingly, no one who heard the boy laughed. This Husker stuff was important. Those candies had been in the very hands of Brook Berringer. Many wished that they had those M & Ms to keep for themselves.

Such adulation is not at all rare. The previous November I had borrowed Brook's truck to pick up a supply of books from my publisher, Gordon Thiessen, in Grand Island, Nebraska. It was late when I got there, having watched the first half of the Florida-Florida State game with Brook. The next morning Gordon said to his son, "Josh, you missed it last night. Art Lindsay came out to pick up some books, and he was using Brook Berringer's truck."

"And you didn't wake me?" Josh protested.

"No, Brook wasn't here," Gordon explained.

"I understand that," Josh replied sorrowfully, "but I could've seen his truck!"

Even more than the enjoyment of the fans, Brook made it to as many of the more than 30 basketball engagements Ott scheduled because of the camaraderie he felt with the other players. Those guys were like family. They were important to him, and he realized that soon there would be a parting of the ways and some of them would not meet again.

He was especially excited about the last game on the schedule to be played in his hometown of Goodland on April 11. He was proud that eight of the guys he'd built relationships with for five years were willing to make the long trip out to extreme western Kansas. Brook even arranged a small plane and pilot to fly some of them out and back. Linebacker Doug Colman, himself a hulking 240-pounder, made the flight. "We were pretty cramped into this plane, and it was kind of scary," he said. "In fact, Clester Johnson and Tony Veland were so scared they decided to take a car back. It was spooky."

About 1,500 people showed up for the fund-raiser, which was played in the same gymnasium where Brook had averaged over 17 points a game in his senior year of high school on Goodland's state qualifying team. More than a basketball game, it was a homecoming celebration for one of the town's true heroes. A hero who never changed from the "good ole Brook" many had known for 20 years. One reason he was so popular in his hometown was that success never went to his head. He always thought of other people, especially the kids. He was sort of a Pied Piper.

Also, since his mother, at one time or another, had many of the children in her elementary school class, the kids always felt Brook was part of their family. When Brook would stop in unannounced to visit his mom's classroom, Jan made the comment, "You could hear a pin drop. The kids would get all shy and then finally one of them would walk up to Brook and size themselves up to him. To them, he was huge."

Two days after the basketball game, Brook appeared on a live radio call-in show at the Cowboy Loop, a restaurant/convenience store local attraction, managed by Brook's good friend, Dax Hayden. His 1994 Orange Bowl jersey was framed and hung in the store as he signed autographs for the fans. The Loop sits at the south end of Main Street where the town kids turn their cars and pickups around in a years-old tradition called "dragging Main."

Excitement ran high that morning as Brook answered questions from a variety of callers, most of whom chose to talk about his victories, rather than the disappointments of the 1995 season.

This was the first time Brook had spent more than a day at home since the football season ended. People were especially interested in his opinion on the NFL draft. He answered the same questions over and over patiently. "I'd prefer to play in Denver or Kansas City," he said, "because of their location. But several coaches, from the Washington Redskins and the New England Patriots have expressed interest."

But he took one woman completely by surprise when she offered an opinion, "Next Saturday is really going to be a great weekend for you." (Referring to the NFL draft.)

"Yeah," Brook quipped with a smile, "my sister's going to have her baby."

CHAPTER 19

A FINAL TOUCH-AND-GO

It was after midnight and into the wee morning hours of Thursday, April 18, when Brook arrived back in Lincoln after spending the entire day with his sister, Nicoel, and then a late dinner with Tiffini. Messages and phone calls awaited his arrival and after sleeping in a little that morning, Brook faced the remainder of the day refreshed and with anticipation.

Wendell Conover, the state director of FCA, had called wanting to know if Brook could do an interview prior to their banquet that night. Brook was scheduled to be one of the speakers at the annual Fellowship of Christian Athletes Lincoln Banquet being held at the Devaney Center that evening. Vince Erickson, a local television sportscaster, wanted to do a live interview at the Devaney Center on on his sports program prior to the banquet. Brook agreed to the interview.

Ron Brown was also trying to contact Brook, wanting to know if Brook could go with him to speak to some schools in Omaha later that day. Ron knew he loved talking to kids–there was nothing he enjoyed more. But with Tobey, Tiffini's brother, in town, a much needed weight training workout waiting for him to tackle and the FCA banquet that night, Brook did not want to overcommit himself.

He was looking forward to the FCA banquet. He saw it as a great opportunity for him to share his faith just two days ahead of the NFL draft.

After checking out several matters on campus that morning,

Brook spent about 45 minutes in the weight room around noon. Then he made a call to Lori Johnson, a Fairbury artist, whom he wanted to do a drawing of his old friend Juke. "I have plenty of videos and pictures of him for you to work from," he assured her.

She agreed to pick them up from him later.

He then ate lunch with former Husker teammate Chad Stanley, and UNL Associate Director of Academic Programs, Keith Zimmer. After lunch, Brook stopped in quickly to see Jeff Schmahl, who works with the university's HuskerVision Network, and then hurried home to meet Tobey so they could take a quick flight over the rolling countryside. They climbed into Tobey's pickup. It was a gorgeous afternoon . . . brilliant sunshine; no jacket needed.

It took only 15 minutes to drive out to the tiny grass airstrip east of Raymond. He and Tobey checked the condition of the 1946 Piper Cub and fueled it. Brook loved the little two-seater which he had flown so often. It was a simple, efficient craft.

As was his habit, he probably went through his preflight checklist and revved-up the motor to test it. As they taxied into the wind the plane wobbled and bounced on the rough strip, just as always. Brook probably felt a stir of excitement, the thrill of every pilot as he is about to leave the pull of earth for the uplift of being in flight. No doubt a smile of pleasure burst across his face as the craft eased into the sky.

He banked the plane to the right, across Raymond Road as it reached 250 feet. Suddenly it was no longer under his control. The right wing dipped swiftly and the aircraft spun into a nose-dive. There was no way to pull it up.

In less time than it takes to tell it, two bodies crashed to the ground; life, as judged in human terms, ended. Flames erupted and consumed the wreckage.

From an eternal perspective, for Brook Berringer, it was but a touch-and-go; amazingly swift, and so unexpected. When he stretched his long legs into that Piper Cub at 2:10, he didn't realize that at 2:20 he would fly through the thin veil that separates time and eternity, the here from the hereafter. Yet he was prepared for that eventuality.

The touch to earth hurt, but Brook was no stranger to pain; for a lifetime, he knew exactly how to process it into gain. But this time he did not have to wait for the result—it was immediate—secured by his commitment to Christ on August 24, 1995.

Therefore, the go was glorious. A total release into the very presence of God, his Father Almighty. True for the thief on a cross, true also for Brook. "... Today you will be with me in paradise" (Luke 23:43). "Death has been swallowed up in victory" (1 Corinthians 15:54).

Every time the telephone rang that afternoon I thought it was the expected call from Brook. He was supposed to have phoned me early in the afternoon with the number of extra tickets he needed for the FCA Banquet. The call never came. Instead, it was about 4:30 when my colleague, Tom Cook, anxiously told me, "Ron Brown needs to talk to you. He says it's urgent."

"Ron, what can I do for you?" I asked hesitantly.

"Art, I think I have bad news. It's Brook."

My heart leaped to my throat.

"It isn't confirmed, but a plane went down, and we think Brook was in it. Do you know if he saw a dentist in Omaha?"

"No, I'm sure his dentist is Roger Plooster, just next door," I answered, numb at the thought.

"Do you think he has dental records?"

"I can run over and find out," I promised.

"Listen, this isn't confirmed. I'll call you back right away, as soon as I know anything."

Tom Cook wanted to know what was going on, but I couldn't speak it for fear it was true.

I rushed next door and called the office manager, Margie Lucchino, aside so no one else could hear. I told her the frightening possibility and asked if they had Brook's dental records. When she said they did, I told her I'd come back as soon as I had further word.

Fifteen minutes later Ron called back, "Art, we still don't know for certain. But can you bring Brook's dental records down to the stadium?"

"I'll be there in 10 minutes," I said as my voice quivered.

Margie had the folder in hand and gave it to me while still trying to calm the dental staff with the hope that nothing had been confirmed.

At the stadium, words would not come easily to the lips of anyone. It was mostly by common consent that Coaches Brown, Gill, Solich, and I got into the van with Tom Osborne for the drive to the crash sight.

The unconfirmed reports of Brook and Tobey's deaths spread like wildfire throughout the world—even as far as Bali, Indonesia. One of Jan's friends in Bali heard the news at the same time that Brook's death was officially confirmed to Jan. A reporter stated that the "pending notification of relatives" courtesy could not be extended to people as well-known as Brook because the public has to know. Unfortunately, Jan Berringer's family will no doubt suffer for a lifetime due to the media's "right-to-know" policy.

Nicoel's husband, Kevin, was planning on staying late at the hospital to catch up on paperwork that evening. However, he called Nicoel to say, "Nicoel, I feel like I need to be home with you tonight; so I'm on my way."

They were both excited about their first child which was due to arrive in two days. They were also excited about the upcoming NFL draft, so they took their plates into the living room to watch for any draft updates. After turning on the TV, Kevin caught the end of a story about the NFL Combine.

Suddenly, a picture of Brook's face loomed across the screen. Nicoel yelled with excitement, "Turn it up, turn it up!"

Nicoel and Kevin, expecting a report about the upcoming draft, were shocked when ESPN continued with a story about a fatal airplane crash near Lincoln. "Tragedy strikes the Cornhuskers. Brook Berringer was killed in a plane crash today . . ."

The two were stunned by the news about Brook. Kevin grabbed Nicoel, sat her down and tried as best as he could to comfort her. He then immediately called Jan, concerned that she might see the same report.

At about the same time in Manhattan, Kansas, Drue had just returned to her sorority house after her last afternoon class. She greeted the unexpected gathering of girls in her room. "Hi, guys? What's going on?"

Her friends, who had seen the news reports, fell silent. When they realized that Drue hadn't heard of her brother's accident, one of them insisted that she call home.

"Why? What's the matter?" Drue implored.

"Just call home," her friend persisted, knowing that this information should come from her mother.

As the girls abruptly left the room for Drue to make the call home, they cried for the pain they knew their friend was about to endure.

Jan's sister, Judy, was at the Berringers' house that afternoon having volunteered to help Jan clean the house and prepare the food for the NFL draft party on Sunday. Judy answered the phone when Tom Osborne first tried to contact Brook's mother about the accident.

When Jan arrived home from school a short time later, Judy ran out to the driveway to meet her.

"Tom Osborne just called and he's going to call you back here in a minute. Come on in the house," Judy said apprehensively.

Jan speculated that he must be calling to wish the family good luck in the draft.

Judy quickly dispelled that notion with the extremely worried look on her face.

"Is there anything wrong?" Jan asked.

"Well, there might be. It sounded like there was an accident."

"Oh no! Brook didn't blow his elbow or knee out while he was working out, did he?"

"I don't know. He said he would call you back in a few minutes."

As soon as they came into the house, the phone rang. Jan immediately answered it and recognized Coach Osborne's voice. She could tell he was on a cellular phone due to the background noise.

"Jan, I just called to tell you that there has been an accident and we don't know if Brook has any involvement in this. We're going to see if he was involved."

Any thoughts of the accident being a football injury vanished.

He went on, "The accident happened outside of town here."

Jan's immediate thoughts were that Brook had a wreck in the pickup. "What kind of accident are you talking about?"

"Airplane," he stated.

Jan's heart hit the floor.

He told her it was an airplane that Brook often flew but that others also flew the plane and he would call back as soon as he knew anything more. Before they hung up, Jan asked how many people had been in the plane, and Tom told her there were two.

"Oh, Tobey was with him," she thought. She quickly told herself that it wasn't Brook. Then she asked the most difficult question, "What is their condition?"

"I'm afraid it's a fatal accident," Tom said as gently as he could.

As soon as she hung up the phone, she began praying as hard as she could. She started pacing and thinking that while she didn't want bad news for any other family, she prayed it wasn't Brook. Her thoughts were interrupted by a phone call from her son-in-law, Kevin.

He told Jan about the news story that he and Nicoel had just seen on ESPN. She now had fewer doubts that it was Brook and Tobey in that airplane. Nevertheless, she told Kevin that nothing had been confirmed and that she didn't think that it was Brook. Hearing Nicoel's cries in the background, Jan asked how she was doing.

"She's just terrible right now and I've got to take care of her so I'll talk to you later. Call us as soon as you hear anything."

As quickly as Jan hung up the phone, it rang again. This time it was Drue.

"Mom! What's going on? How's Nicoel? Is there anything wrong?"

Afraid that Drue had also seen the news story, Jan asked her what she knew.

Drue was very distraught and thought that Nicoel had just lost her baby. Jan assured her that the baby was fine but she knew that the truth was not going to make Drue feel any better.

When she hung up the telephone, Jan noticed a police car was pulling into the driveway. She ran down the hallway telling Judy to get rid of whoever was in the car. She didn't want to hear anything they had to say. After Judy let the Goodland Chief of Police in the front door, she determined Jan would have to face the visitors. Judy walked down the hallway to the locked bathroom door and urged her to come out.

Jan, realizing she couldn't delay the inevitable, came to the living room to hear what the policeman had to say.

"We're here to report an accident. It's not confirmed yet."

"I know. You don't need to tell me anything. I'm waiting for a telephone call from Tom Osborne."

As the policemen were getting ready to leave, they said they were going to tell Ruth Lake, Tobey's mother, about the unconfirmed accident. Jan urged them to wait while she collected her thoughts on the best way to inform Tobey's mother of the tragic news.

She thought it would be best to let Troy, Tobey's older brother, describe how it should be handled. After unsuccessfully trying to obtain Troy's unlisted phone number, the operator agreed to attempt to contact Troy and give him a message to call the Chief of Police as soon as possible. As they were impatiently waiting for Troy's return call, the phone rang. It was Ruth Lake. With panic in her voice, she asked Jan what was going on.

Jan thought that maybe Ruth had seen the report on television.

"What do you know?" she asked cautiously.

"Troy's wife just called me and asked why the Goodland Chief of Police wanted to talk to Troy?"

Jan's best intentions had backfired and now she had to be the one to tell Ruth about the accident. She told her that it was still unconfirmed and urged her to pray hard that it wasn't them.

Before the police left the Berringer house, Jan had one final question for them.

"Was there a vehicle there?"

"Yes."

"Was it a brown pickup?"

"It was a Colorado pickup licensed to Tobey Lake."

Her prayers changed at that moment. They were no longer for the survival of Brook and Tobey but for the strength of their families. In one brief moment, Jan Berringer had gone from planning an NFL draft party to preparing the funeral of her only son.

As she began making the necessary arrangements she never dreamed she would have to make, Brook's younger Brittany Spaniel, Bodie, slowly moved toward Brook's hunting jacket that had been left on the back of a chair. Bodie tugged at the jacket, pulled it to the floor and laid there on the jacket the rest of the day. Everyone was going to miss Brook.

The sheriff's department had the crash site well secured, although numerous reporters and photographers were already on the scene when we arrived shortly after five. None of us had any desire to leave the van as we stared at the twisted wreckage. The flash fire after impact had consumed most of the aircraft; there was nothing to see. We gave the dental records to Sheriff Wagner for the pathologist to use and turned away. We stopped across the road at the airstrip. The attendant, without really saying so, confirmed our worst fears.

All across Nebraska and Kansas there are thousands of people who remember exactly where they were, what they were doing, when they first heard the shocking news. Family, friends, fans, regardless of age, sex or race were torn to tears at the thought of the unbelievable, hoping against hope that what they'd heard wasn't true.

It was nearly six o'clock when the coaches and I got back to Lincoln. I had no desire to change into something casual for the FCA Banquet, that gala affair which was supposed to start in half-an-hour. I headed directly for the Devaney Center. For a couple of blocks I thought to myself, "It could've been someone else in that plane. Brook could still meet me at 6:15."

But as quickly as the thought entered my head, I dismissed it as unworthy of this finest of young men. He'd want me, and everyone to face this with courage, just as he handled every difficulty that came his way. It was obvious that he was gone. Now came the task of dealing with it.

The cavernous Devaney Center was rather quiet when I walked in. Preparations for the evening were nearly complete. Guests were just beginning to wander in.

When they caught sight of me, FCA friends who knew of the close relationship between Brook and me, and who had heard the news, came to greet me with an embrace and tears. I fumbled at words to confirm what I knew. I was on the brink of deep sorrow, ready to tumble in.

Then Dr. Steve Carveth, who hadn't heard the news greeted me, "Art, have you had a good day?"

"No," I replied quietly. "It's been a hard day."

He gave me a questioning look, since I always try to be upbeat.

As he turned away, God graciously intervened. I knew instantly that though what I had heard and seen in the last two hours was unfathomable and unwanted, it was at the same time one of the most glorious, glad days of my life. Brook Berringer, whom I and so many others loved dearly, was home! I could not wish him back into this world for anything.

Brook was supposed to have joined his teammates, Mike Minter, Tony Veland, Aaron Graham and Aaron Penland on the program that night, along with Nebraska Receivers Coach Ron Brown and Head Coach Tom Osborne.

Prior to the banquet, the FCA planned to present each speaker a copy of the painting called "Influence." This picture has represented the positive influence that athletes have had in our society for the past 30 years. The portraits were placed in front of the speaker's podium before the banquet began. The "Influence" picture shows a young boy wearing an oversized football jersey. The boy is grasping a football and looking toward a group of older athletes sitting in a circle discussing their faith. The young boy's jersey is No. 18. It didn't take long for many of the people who attended the banquet to make the connection between Brook and the portraits.

Ironically, Arch Unruh, who painted the "Influence" portrait was the twin brother of Duane. It was Duane Unruh who had been Warren Berringer's high school football coach, and would later help Brook decide which college to attend.

Shortly after I arrived, Ron Brown asked me, "Art, you know I was supposed to interview Brook this evening about his relationship with Christ. Do you think you could give his testimony for him?"

A tear tried to choke out my voice as I responded, "As long as I'm able to bite my lip enough times."

By the time the other athletes and coaches had finished their part of the program, I had gained control of myself. I realized that I had the responsibility to speak for Brook who could no longer speak for himself.

Ron was gracious in his introduction. "The greatest news about Brook Berringer is that less than a year ago he trusted his life to Jesus Christ. He trusted Jesus Christ for eternal life so that he could live with him forever and ever. In a sense he died at that moment; and a new life was given to him in Christ, and he had the pleasure, the last few months, of walking with Christ Jesus. And now he's in a spot we long to be in–those of us who know Jesus as Savior and Lord.

"I would like a very special guest to come and speak on behalf of Brook. Art used to send me letters to give to Brook. I wouldn't open the letters, but I knew what was in them. I knew they were just packed with wisdom and truth from the Bible that the Lord had given him to share with Brook. I want him to come and share with you a little bit about that."

As I walked to the podium, I was strengthened in the knowledge that the accompanying applause was not for me, but in honor of Brook. I had carefully crafted my opening words, then let the rest flow freely.

I told the audience of over 1,000 people about the night of August 24, 1995, when Brook finally understood what it meant to trust Christ with his life. I told them about the sin problem that everyone has and what the Bible says is the penalty for those sins.

But then I also shared the good news that Jesus paid that penalty with his own life, that we each might experience salvation and a new life in Christ.

That new life was appealing to Brook. In fact that's probably why 2 Corinthians 5:17 meant so much to him. It says, "Therefore, if anyone is in Christ, he is a new creation, the old has gone, the new has come!"

I also shared about the time I asked Brook what we really wanted to see happen over the next four to five years. His response was that he simply wanted to grow in his relationship with Jesus Christ because it was the greatest thing that had ever happened to him. While I was thinking of the temporal, Brook was thinking of the eternal.

"The beauty of this young man's life. Wow! Isn't it marvelous that God can accomplish so much in one young life in just 22 years, 23 this July 9th. What a tremendous, tremendous challenge he gives to us! I'm just thrilled beyond words this evening.

"If any of you, any of you who knew him, want to ever see him again you have to go to heaven. That's where Brook is.

"Praise God for the delight of this young man, who knew what he wanted; and more than anything else, he wanted to glorify Christ in his life.

"God bless you."

Ron stepped forward immediately and said, "Thank you, Art. Thank you very much for your faithfulness in being God's instrument not only in Brook's life, but in my life, and so many other lives. We appreciate all you do."

"You know, the death of a great person should add life to those he leaves behind. Certainly that's true of Brook Berringer.

"But it's also true with Jesus Christ, the Son of God. He gave us life, not only for this life, but for eternal life.

"Some of you may be wondering, 'What does all this mean? How does it translate in my own life?'

"I used to run on this track team in New York. I paid my dues to be on the team and got my nice uniform. But when they held meets, if there were open slots in the race, anyone could jump in and run–you didn't have to be a member of the team. In one particular race, two members of our track team lined up for the 100-meter dash and there two open spots. A couple of guys from the streets that nobody knew, with their old raggedy sweats, jumped in there.

"The gun went off and everyone expected the two guys from our track team to win the race handily because they were trained runners. But, lo and behold, these two guys from the team finished three and four.

"I thought, 'Wow! I wonder who these guys are?' So I looked in the newspaper the next day for the results. But those two guys from the street weren't even listed. The guys from our team were listed one and two. So I asked a friend, 'Why didn't those guys from the street show up in the results?'

"My friend said, 'Well, if you're not on the team your race doesn't count.'

"And you know, there are a lot of people in the game of life who are running fast. They may look good in all that they're doing. They're moving up ahead in their careers. They're scoring touchdowns. They're winning championships. They're well thought of. They're the biggest in their class. They have the best grades. They're the nicest looking. They're popular. They have all the support of their friends. They grew up on the right side of the tracks.

"But it would be a sad day, one day, when you stand before the Lord God—and everyone in this room will do it—and He says, 'Even though you ran faster than anybody else on earth, your race doesn't count because you didn't join the team.'

"So the question tonight is simply this: are you on God's team? Have you done what all these athletes have talked about tonight? Have you trusted in Jesus Christ alone for eternal life?

"Or is this just another night when we've heard a few sermons, and got to see, as you would define them, some celebrity athletes. Is it a life changing experience for you? Life is very brief, as we've seen today. None of us are promised tomorrow. There's no guarantee tonight that you'll even make it home. You don't know when God is going to say, 'Look, I told you a hundred times about me. I've given you so many times to listen to what's being said about my son Jesus Christ; and you continue to reject Him. You continually turn the other ear because you're in some mad pursuit for something on this earth.'

"And you're foolish. You're a foolish person. Because if there's any person in this building tonight who would dare walk out of here without knowing Jesus Christ as their Savior and Lord, without knowing the only insurance plan that exists, then perhaps, perhaps we have to consider ourselves foolish.

"The cross of Jesus Christ points the finger at everyone of us right now and says, 'You can't run from me anymore.'

"Tonight you can put your faith in Him, and in Him alone; and trust your life to Jesus Christ and have a home in heaven reserved for you for ever and ever and ever and ever! And nothing will ever get in the way of it! Not a plane crash! Nothing!"

CHAPTER 20

IN LASTING HONOR

K GBI, an Omaha radio station, broadcast and rebroadcast that portion of the banquet (as highlighted in the previous chapter). The station had more requests for that half hour on the air and for Brook's testimony from December 29th than for anything in its previous 50-year history.

In reporting his death, normally tough-minded sportscasters were moved to tears and sportswriters stumbled over a plethora of adjectives to try to describe the indescribable essence of who this sports star was. Newspapers across the United States told the story; ESPN aired a special tribute; *Sports Illustrated* did a two-page spread; and on the floor of the United States Senate presidential candidate Bob Dole affirmed, "Brook was a champion in all aspects of his life."

At the same time, fans, thousands upon thousands of them, watched re-run footage of Brook in football highlights, in hunting gear as he walked the fields with his dogs, holding hands with a patient in a hospital, reading *Green Eggs and Ham* to school children. Longingly they searched for a glimpse of who he was, something by which to identify this man who suddenly, in the midst of tragedy, loomed bigger than life.

In thoughtful consideration, an anonymous fan taped two roses and a one-word farewell message, "Love," on the window of the South Stadium entrance.

On Monday, April 22, it seemed as if the whole town of Goodland, Kansas, had shut down to mourn the loss and celebrate the lives of Brook Berringer and Tobey Lake. More than 4,000 gathered in the Max L. Jones Fieldhouse for a funeral service. Just 10 days before, Brook had participated in his last athletic event in that facility–the last basketball game played by seniors of the Cornhusker football team. Brook had wowed his hometown fans with a game high 26 points and three monstrous dunks as the event raised nearly $5,000 for the Goodland Activities Center. Little did they know the true, lasting significance of their thunderous standing ovation for their local hero.

KFAB, an Omaha radio station, broadcast the entire three-hour funeral service live. The requests were so great that it was repeated in its entirety the next evening.

Personally, I think I shall never forget the expression of serenity I saw on the faces of more than 100 Berringer relatives in that auditorium. Certainly many of them had been through an emotional wringer, especially those whose first word of Brook's death was from a news flash.

But I saw a strength in the faces of the Berringers which was a true honor and testimony to Brook. They understood, in the midst of deep sorrow, that they had come together primarily to celebrate, to honor the life of the one they had loved, nurtured, and prized.

Their grieving was not over. Surely the loss would be felt for a long time to come. But inwardly they were determined to live all the more fully in testimony to the contribution Brook had made in their lives.

Mark Miller, Dax Hayden, Devlin Mull, Chris Wilson, Tony Veland, Phil Ellis, Clester Johnson and Brad Wells served as pallbearers.

Brook's lasting legacy was in the lives he touched. I could literally see it in the expression on their faces.

Brook's mother, Jan, had asked that Tom Osborne, Turner Gill, Ron Brown, and I speak for Brook. Then his uncle, Stan Ellis, was to add words of appreciation from the family.

In summary, Coach Osborne remembered Brook as a loyal, honest, and courageous person. "I've coached some 2,000 football players at Nebraska," he said. "And I can honestly say nobody I ever coached had better character than Brook Berringer. He was transparent in the best sense of the word.

"I'm certainly a better person for having known him."

He went on to describe Brook, by his standards, as a success. "There are two questions you have to ask yourself. One, what did you do with what you had? On that count, Brook was a success. As a student and as an athlete, he got as much as he could out of himself. The second, did you honor God with what you were given? Again, I think Brook did a great job with that. He honored God in the way he operated; everything he did. So, as far as I'm concerned, the quality of his life was excellent–no regrets."

Coach Gill read a letter he had written to Brook, in which he focused on Brook's talents on the field as well as how he carried himself in public. "Not only were you one of the most talented quarterbacks ever to play at Nebraska, but you demonstrated the true definition of a team player. You were very unselfish. You uplifted other players. You did all things with such grace, dignity and poise.

"I'm so proud to have coached you. I'm so proud to have known you. Not only were you a great role model as a football player, but you were a great example of how to live your life for Christ.

"You put everything you had into everything you did: whether it was pursuing academics, athletics, loving nature, being a friend, helping others, or just having fun.

"If we could all have the zest for life that you had, the world would be an amazing place.

"If I had thought a person could get to heaven by being a good person then I would have believed you were going there all along; for you were truly a good person with a gift for helping others. However, the Bible tells us that the only way to get to heaven is by believing that Jesus died for all of our sins.

"I saw such goodness in your life and I hoped that you were saved. But I did not know of your salvation until the day you came into my office and told me. I cannot tell you the feeling I felt when I knew that you had given your life to Christ and that I would see you again in heaven. Your life on earth was such an inspiration to all of us who wish to glorify Jesus.

"You must feel such joy now, looking down and seeing how many people you have touched. I love you, Brook, and I will miss you until we meet again. Save me a place. I'll be there someday."

Coach Ron Brown had gotten very well acquainted with the Berringer family during the recruiting process in 1991 and was deeply impressed, not only with Brook's athletic ability, but also with his cordial and thoughtful approach to life as a person. "He was a very unassuming guy," Coach Brown explained, "a guy with great talent, yet very humble and really appreciated the finer things of life.

"That ability, as you all know, came to the forefront in 1994 when Brook entered the scene and became a national hero and helped lead our football team to a national championship as the starting quarterback.

"But, perhaps what was even more meaningful to me, were the letters that were sent from a gentleman who's on the platform here, named Arthur Lindsay. He sent me the letters to give to Brook, and those letters had tremendous wisdom and insight about life; and most importantly his love for Brook and his desire to share Jesus Christ with Brook. Brook always told me he loved those letters.

"On August 24, 1995, Brook Berringer made the most important decision of his life, according to him. As Turner just mentioned, he had trusted in Jesus Christ as his Savior and Lord, trusted Him for eternal life. Brook was never one of those guys you push into something; you don't force something on him, and he's not a very pushy person. He grasps information, he ponders it, he chews on it and thinks about it very thoroughly.

"One day, in the middle of the season, in our weight room which has been a haven for informal conversations between coaches and players, I had a great talk with Brook Berringer. He said, 'Coach Brown, when I decided to trust Jesus Christ as my Savior and Lord it was the greatest thing that I've ever done in my life. I'm so excited.'

"And we know how excited he got about flying and hunting and fishing and throwing touchdown passes. But this was the most momentous day of his life.

"Jesus Christ offers the gift of eternal life. But a gift, for it to count, not only has to be presented, it also has to be received. That's when the transaction is completed; and that's what Brook did, he made that completion. It doesn't count as a completion until it's caught. Brook made the greatest catch of his life on August 24, 1995.

"If I had a question for Brook right now it might be, 'Brook, if it were possible, would you come back? Would you come back to see us, your friends and your family, and all your teammates who loved you so much? Would you come back to see your dear mom who has raised you by herself for the most part, and your sisters—your older sister and her baby that is about to be born? Would you come back and see us?

"I think Brook would say, 'Without any lack of respect to you, Coach Brown, and all of you—not on your life! I wouldn't come back because right now, right now I'm with my earthly father whom I haven't seen in years. And most importantly I'm with my Heavenly Father, whom I've heard so much about, and I was ready to see!'

"I think there's a greater question; the one Brook would ask to every single one of us right now, and that is: 'Are you prepared?'

"Are you prepared to die? If we're not prepared to die, we're not prepared to live.

"You see God has allowed Brook to throw *one final pass*—today—to us. The question is simply this: will we receive it? Brook Berringer lives eternally and there's only one way we're going to get to see Brook Berringer again. That is, we must go to heaven to see him because that's where he lives."

In preparing my own remarks for that day, because of limited time allowed, I spent more effort in refining what I wanted to say than anything I've done in years. Now, I trim it some more.

"I have only a few minutes in which to honor the finest man I've ever known, who honored me with his friendship. I can do that only by honoring what was most important to him, Jesus Christ.

"Brook Warren Berringer was my prayer partner. We shared deeply, intimately in matters of the Spirit. Let me share just four events from the last month.

"But first I must preface that with something Brook said last October, a testimony as pure and beautiful as anything I've ever heard. We had just finished our weekly Bible study and I asked him, 'Brook, what do you really want?' "What do you want to see happen in the next 4 or 5 years?"

I went on to relay Brook's response and his eternal perspective as I had shared at the FCA Banquet earlier in the week. It was underscored by his favorite scripture verse, 2 Corinthians 5:17, 'Therefore, if anyone is in Christ Jesus, he is a new creation: the old has gone, the new has come.'

I then continued by telling about the time I asked Brook if he would help me, as a sounding board, proofread a novel I was writing. He agreed.

"Four weeks ago a very beautiful scene emerged in that story and I shared it with Brook to get his reaction.

"The parallel to last Thursday is astounding.

"In the novel, Andy, a very dedicated Christian, has just been informed by his pastor of the death of his wife and daughter, burned beyond recognition in a trailer fire. Andy, filled with doubts and questions finally said to the preacher, 'I don't suppose it would make any sense to ask why?'

"In a flash of inspiration, Pastor White said, 'No, Andy, that wouldn't make any sense. But the joy we have as Christians is that although we might not always know the *whys* of life we do know the Who of life and He is the one who makes all the difference!'

"When he looked up from reading I asked him, 'Does that make sense?'

"Brook answered, 'Art, that's great!'

"For anyone here this afternoon who is trying to ask, 'Why?' let me assure you, I don't know. But I can assure you absolutely that Brook Berringer knew the *who*. And I rejoice in that."

I then told the gathering about what turned out be our last Bible study together on the Thursday before Easter. We had shared communion together and I had focused the study to relate to the upcoming NFL draft. The first scripture from our study was:

1 Peter 2:9, 'But you are a chosen people, a royal priesthood, a holy nation, a people belonging to God, that you may declare the praises of him who called you out of darkness into his wonderful light.'

"And Brook agreed with me that afternoon, that the No. 1 purpose for being drafted would be to bring glory to God." I continued.

"Praise God who sees and knows more than we can ever comprehend.

"Indeed! Brook was drafted.

"He is the No. 1 draft pick of 1996.

"Brook was especially preparing for a position on that team. He started memorizing God's Playbook last August. He would ask me from time to time, what was the next verse I had for him. This was the next verse I had for him. It is so awesome.

Philippians 3:14, 'I press on toward the goal to win the prize for which God has called me heavenward in Christ Jesus.'

"Ha! He beat us all home.

"Way to go Brook! I've said it a thousand times and I'll say it again, 'Man, I'm so proud of you!'

"Four weeks ago Brook asked me about a book I gave him for Valentine's Day, Oswald Chambers' classic, *My Utmost for His Highest*, a collection of daily devotions. He wanted to know what time I read the daily passage; and I told him it depended on circumstances. He said that he preferred to read it first thing in the morning.

"Last Friday afternoon it suddenly dawned on me: the last thing Brook would have read before going off to the weight room and then off to flying would have been the lesson for April 18. Let me read the last paragraph:

Be ready for the sudden surprise visits of God. A ready person never needs to get ready. Think of the time we waste trying to get ready when God has called! The burning bush is a symbol of everything that surrounds the ready soul, it is ablaze with the presence of God.

"Praise God! I've never known anyone more ready.

"Anyone here today who would like to see Brook Berringer again I can tell you exactly where he is.

"That plane crash did not destroy Brook Berringer. It was just a touch-and-go.

"About six weeks ago, Brook and I talked about the certainty of death. I told him, 'Brook, if you hear that I've died, don't you dare cry. Just praise God, because the only reason I'm living in this world is to get out of it successfully.'

"I've had to eat those words.

"Brook, I apologize for my countless, selfish tears of anguish.

"But I praise God, praise God, praise God!

"Well done, Dear Friend! Welcome home!

"I hope that everyone here today will say, through faith in Jesus Christ. 'Hey! Brook! Save me a place. I'm coming too!'"

Brook's uncle, Stan Ellis, from Indianapolis, who had always been a stable spiritual influence in Brook's life, had the difficult task of speaking a response on behalf of the family. He spoke of the choices all of us must make: "of attitude, of faith. And Brook would want us to think about that these days.

"Brook never walked through life. He ran. When he would open one Christmas present, he always had his eye on the next one. He had to ride that bicycle at three.

"His life was always, as you've heard, 'What's next!' He was planning to ride with the Blue Angels if he could work that out. He was always out there ready for something more.

"He just couldn't wait. We have to.

"Having accomplished more in 22 years than many have achieved in their allotted 70 years here on earth, Brook went on to a reunion with his dad and his Savior."

A four-minute highlight video was shown of Brook: hunting with his dogs, talking to children, playing in the Orange Bowl and throwing picture-perfect passes. His No. 18 football helmet sat atop his casket.

Mark Miller and his accompanist from "*Sawyer Brown*" were on hand to sing Brook's favorite country song, "I'll Leave the Light on."

Troy Lake read the following poem, as a tribute to the two men who had a common passion for flying:

High Flight

Oh, I have slipped the surly bonds of Earth,
And danced the skies on laughter-silvered wings:
Sunward I've climbed and joined the tumbling mirth
Of sun-split clouds–and done a hundred things
You have not dreamed of–wheeled and soared and swung
High in the sunlit silence.
Hovering there
I've chased the shouting wind along and flung
My eager craft through footless halls of air.
Up, up the long, delirious, burning blue
I've topped the wind-swept heights with easy grace,
Where never lark, or even eagle flew;
And, while with silent, lifting mind I've trod
The high untrespassed sanctity of space,
Put on my hand, and touched the face of God.

By John Gillespie Magee, Jr. 19, an American Volunteer in the Royal Canadian Air Force who was killed in action December 11, 1941.

Later, hundreds of mourners stood five or six deep around the green canopy in the middle of the cemetery under which lay the polished wood coffin adorned only by his Nebraska Cornhusker football helmet. Brook's cousins stood ready, each with a single red rose for a final touch of remembrance.

EPILOGUE

From the very first moment that people heard about Brook Berringer being killed in an airplane crash–once they got past the initial shock, and truth began to set in–the impact he had on lives was more powerful than ever. In many cases, it was an instantaneous decision; a commitment to get into life where Brook had left it.

For years, this outstanding young man had wielded a great, positive influence on everyone who met him, and on countless others who watched his career with appreciation from a distance. He was the best known "backup quarterback" in college football. People just naturally admired the manner in which Brook fulfilled his role . . . quietly, efficiently, often painfully. He stood as a role model in the purest sense, and men and women and children who met him casually–in a restaurant or a school, at a gun club or the movies, outside the stadium, wherever–always spoke of him afterwards in personal terms, as if they were good friends.

Even people who never met him thought of him as a friend, someone special. That's just the kind of person he was–no pretensions. What you saw is what you got.

In spite of his notoriety and his good looks, Brook was a very private person. He graciously gave himself to others in public situations, but did not try to grab the spotlight to draw attention to himself. On the contrary, the opposite was true. Frequently, he avoided sportswriters' interviews; and seldom did he read what they wrote. (Ken Hambleton of the *Lincoln Journal-Star* was a notable exception.) Certainly he wanted to be accepted, just like anyone else. But who he was as a man was far more important to him than what he was as a football player, hunter, fisherman, or pilot.

With his death, therefore, people began to be introduced to who Brook Berringer was. Up until then, they knew they liked what they saw on the outside, though they might not have known why. But when they saw him at last, for the first time, from the inside out, they truly marveled. What they had suspected, but hadn't been able to define was quite true: Brook Berringer was exactly who they always thought he was–genuine.

This revelation of the man has resulted in an untold number of transformed lives beginning from the day Brook went home to be with Christ. Jan Berringer received over 10,000 pieces of mail, a large number of which testified to the great impact Brook's life and death had on each of their own lives.

Many have allowed God to take control of their lives as a result of the testimony of Brook's life at the FCA Banquet the night of April 18. A letter from a young real estate agent in Fremont, Nebraska, is an indication of that initial impact:

> When I found out Brook Berringer was killed in a plane crash I was shocked. How could this Nebraska football player with such a bright future die so young? Growing up in Nebraska I looked up to the players and sometimes probably thought they were invincible. Brook was such a neat guy to see go through the program. He had a great personality, loved kids and was always smiling. When I heard that Brook had accepted the Lord as his Savior I was relieved and this is when I really questioned where I was headed.
>
> On Friday, April 19, my fiancée Michele and I were going out for dinner. I had heard that KGBI was going to air the Fellowship of Christian Athletes meeting from the Thursday night where Brook was supposed to speak. As we were driving to the restaurant we heard Brook's testimony and then heard Art Lindsay and Ron Brown speak at the FCA meeting.

Art said that if anybody wanted to see Brook again they must go to heaven to see him. I thought about that as we sat in the restaurant parking lot; and for the first time found a reason for Brook's death.

The whole time I was hearing this on the radio I was crying about Brook's death, but every word was hitting home. Coach Brown went on to say if you left that building that night without accepting the Lord as your Savior you have a problem with God. I knew that if I went home that night without knowing God that I wouldn't be happy. When Coach Brown invited people at the meeting to accept the Lord I closed my eyes and said that prayer with him. After I did this it was like the weight of the world was lifted off of my shoulders. I thought what a great feeling it is to know that if I died that night I was going to heaven.

That night when I heard how much God has done for me and how much he loves me it was so comforting. I am so thankful that I listened to Coach Brown, Brook, and Art because it changed my life and introduced me to my personal relationship with God. If I could touch half as many people as Brook I would be happy. Like Art said, he is a great loss to us, but a fresh deposit to eternity.

Brook accepted the Lord on August 24, 1995, and I get married August 24, 1996–it will be an even more special day to Michele and me, knowing that.

Wes Wilmer

Tony Veland, a dear friend with whom Brook had shared the disappointment of injuries and the pleasures of success, summed up his own tribute in succinct words, "Brook was a great teammate, a great friend, and a great person. These kinds of things happen unexpectedly. I know Brook's family is hurting and his friends and teammates are hurting. But Brook won the biggest championship of his life when he committed himself to the Lord. Although we mourn, we rejoice for him."

At Wayne State College, in northeast Nebraska, Pam Drickey, a student athlete, had been witnessing to one of her teammates, Amy Broderson, for a long time. Amy loved sports her entire life, especially basketball, playing point guard for the women's team. During the past year she dealt with injury and defeat on the basketball court. Amy realized that basketball was not all there was to life. She began asking Pam questions about God and what role He played in her life. She even took the big step of occasionally attending church.

When Brook died she read every newspaper account she could get her hands on. Several articles said that Brook was a Christian and had made a commitment about a year earlier. God used many other circumstances to get Amy's attention, but Brook's testimony brought her to the brink. On the way home from church, she asked Pam what a commitment was. With that understanding, the two of them prayed together and she made a commitment to Christ of her own.

As Chris Bahl, from the Nebraska Athletic Department, sat there watching the funeral service on April 22nd, he felt his whole world come crashing down on top of him. He had made the long journey down to Goodland on the team bus, wanting to say farewell to a man who had become a close friend over a two-year period. He was certain, in making the trip, that somehow the funeral was to be a special event. However, he heard more than he bargained for. He and Brook had many things in common: both were from Kansas, loved hunting and fishing, and of course, were involved in sports. The impact Brook had on his life had been great.

But the two of them had never talked about Christ. In fact, Chris had never shared with anyone, not even his own parents or his wife, about the deep yearning in his heart to be a man of God. And doubts assailed him because he never really understood what it all meant. Although he considered himself a strong Christian, he felt like an outsider, wanting to get in.

Listening to men, whom he respected greatly, eulogize Brook that afternoon, revealing how much Jesus Christ was the firm foundation of Brook's life, he was deeply stirred. "Right there, it hit me," he shared later. "What Brook had is exactly what I had wanted all my life.

"I was determined not to be a 'closet Christian' any longer. I knew that my old life was over and my life was being born again. I knew that when I left that gym I left the old Chris there–I suppose he's still sitting there.

"I owe that change to Brook. That's the best thing, not only he, but anyone on earth ever did for me."

Clester Johnson was another one of the thousands who sat through the funeral service, badgered by conflicting emotions. On one hand, he felt privileged to be there, honored that his friendship with Brook was so well-known to his mother that she had asked him, along with his good friend Tony Veland, to be a pallbearer. But on the other hand, he wept, as did many of his teammates, when Coach Gill choked up in the midst of his words of tribute.

Clester reflected on the first time he met Brook at the spring game in 1991 before they came on campus in August as aspiring quarterbacks for the Cornhuskers; they instantly liked one another. Clester, having lost his mother at age five, had that extra insight into Brook's pain. Though Brook was quiet and unassuming, Clester respected the big guy from Kansas because he was undaunted by the bevy of candidates for the position. "Brook's goal from day one," he said, "was to be the starting quarterback. He had no desire to play mop-up in the fourth quarter."

Across five years of playing together, their relationship grew strong, even when Clester was transformed into a receiver. Brook, from the relative seclusion of the plains of Kansas, had a lot of questions about blacks–their culture, attitudes and desires. While others avoided such issues, without hesitation, Brook freely asked Clester directly, for example, about the purpose or the rationale behind Black Entertainment Television. Nor was he ashamed to show his ignorance by asking the meaning of phrases commonly used in the black community, or how Clester felt about certain racial issues. Open moments of communication like that served to form a firm bond of understanding between them.

Clester's heart, therefore, was heavy as he listened to the speakers. He had played basketball in that very place with Brook just 10 days earlier. Brook had seemed so alive, so ready for life.

Suddenly it dawned on him, while Ron Brown was speaking, that Brook was yet alive. He recalled to mind what he had heard from his youth that all the answers to life are in Jesus Christ.

Hope began to soften the sadness in his heart.

He was thrilled to hear clearly that Brook had committed his life to Jesus Christ as his personal Savior. "That means," he thought to himself, "Brook is alive forever!"

Quietly then, he too, just as his friend had done eight months earlier, entrusted himself to God's grace in Christ.

On the long drive back to Lincoln he was strengthened by a peace in his spirit he had never known. He told his teammate Steve Ott and Steve's wife, Michelle, of his commitment. "When I go out," he said, "I want to go out like Brook. If I go down like that I wouldn't be afraid.

"I'm in tune now!"

About five weeks before he died, Brook and I were having lunch at Vincenzo's in downtown Lincoln, our last meal together. We spent some time in discussing this book, which we intended to write over the next several years. We agreed that the first chapter would be about the relationship he had with his dad, which was one of the foundational strengths of his life.

Brook said on many occasions, in many different ways, that he felt his dad's presence as he thought about him every day, "When I'm walking in the fields hunting with my bird dogs, I feel that he's right there with me. When I'm in the stadium throwing a touchdown pass I know that my dad has the best seat in the house." Throughout his life he received tremendous comfort in realizing the presence of his father–death was only a temporary separation.

The real essence of what hopefully everyone has learned from Brook's life and death is that memories are only building blocks to the present. If we dwell on the past we're apt to miss the beauty of what God wants to reveal now, next! Today is a fresh present God has laid in our hands. Yesterday's gift is gone. Tomorrow's may not come.

Because of his faith in Jesus Christ, in the eternal sense, Brook is truly alive today. And when we think of him it might help to focus on the present Brook, not the past.

Today, we don't have to ask anything for Brook—he now has it all. I just praise God for the honor of having walked in fellowship with the two of them, trusting God that he will use the continuing testimony of Brook's life to bring glory to Himself—which is the ultimate purpose of every man.

So in a very real sense, death has not silenced Brook Berringer— it has given him a greater platform from which to speak.

On the bus ride back to Lincoln from Goodland after the funeral, I set my heart on the task of writing this book, and finishing it in time for his 23rd birthday on July 9th. I did not want to write the book of a dead man, but to share the passion and vitality of one who is alive forever. I also wanted this book to be Brook's *one final pass* to you, the reader! As Coach Ron Brown has said to those who mourn the loss of Brook, "Are you prepared to receive the pass of salvation (accepting Jesus Christ as Lord and Savior) that God has given Brook the privilege of throwing to you?" It's God message of salvation, but he may have chosen this moment to use Brook's life to touch you.

I now happily conclude with the prayer I'm confident Brook utters for us all:

> The Lord bless you
> and keep you;
> the Lord make his face
> shine upon you
> and be gracious to you;
> the Lord turn his face
> toward you
> and give you peace.
>
> Numbers 6:24-26

BROOK'S MEMORY BANK

Exodus 15:2
Numbers 6:24-26
Joshua 1:8-9
1 Samuel 18:3
Psalms 103:1-3, 119:9-11
Ecclesiastes 4:9-12
Jeremiah 29:11-13
Micah 6:8
Zephaniah 3:17
Matthew 6:33
John 3:16
Romans 3:23, 6:23, 8:28, 10:9
2 Corinthians 5:17
Ephesians 2:8-9
Philippians 3:14
1 John 1:9

15 YEARS LATER

IN JAN'S WORDS

I will always be occupied by my memories of my husband Warren, and of Brook and his two sisters, Nicoel and Drue, growing up. I will never run out of things to think about. As time goes by, now thirty years since Warren has passed away, I am remembering more of the good family times and less of the times of seven years of hospitals, treatment, and Warren suffering from a severe eye injury followed by fighting to survive a very bad kind of cancer. Thankfully, what stands out most about those years of suffering and strife is the ability Warren had to help others deal with their burdens. He was so courageous and kept a positive mind, always showing everyone, especially his children, how to handle the tough times. His strong faith was his foundation for dealing with his struggles and for turning this mountain in his path into something powerfully good. He taught his children how to handle adversity.

No one knows why some people seem to go along with no problems, with their life apparently like a bowl of cherries while others find a big mountain in their path. Ron Brown says that when this happens, you have a choice to make. You can become bitter, throw in the towel, lead a life full of despair. Or you can keep trying to get around that mountain, set your goals on being a source of inspiration to others and learn to overcome your grief and be a positive influence to others.

As I continue to take steps around that mountain that was thrown across my path, sometimes taking two steps forward and one back, I am blessed by the many people I met on the book tour when *One Final Pass* was released. I have vivid memories of times such as a young lady who came to one of the book signing sessions in northeastern Nebraska. She told me that she was devastated by a divorce and how she didn't believe there was any way she could handle the divorce and the thought of rearing her children by herself. After reading *One Final Pass*, she was inspired and is handling the adversity one step at a time around that mountain. I keep her in my thoughts and prayers. All things are possible with God.

I met so many of the good people of Nebraska and heard countless stories on the book tour. I am proud of the impact that Brook's life had on so many. I've received countless letters from people all over the country who took the time and effort to write to me to tell me that they either sought to know the Lord or renewed their faith after reading about Brook's death from this earthly life.

Many college age people wrote to tell me how they watched Nebraska football on TV and only knew Brook through his football life and were so saddened by the news of the accident. They thought about how their own life can be unexpectedly snuffed out in an instant. They wanted me to know that when they read *One Final Pass*, they wanted what Brook had.

Many journeys of seeking or renewing their relationship with the Lord was inspired by the story of my son. I believe Ron Brown is right when he says that it was all part of God's plan. After fifteen years since the accident, I still get letters occasionally telling about the impact that Brook's life and death had on their life or how their children were influenced.

Many tell me about naming their baby after Brook, whether it's a boy or a girl. The Siruta family who live near the Wildlife Refuge that is dedicated to Brook's memory in Clay County, Nebraska, sent me pictures of their triplets, a boy and two girls. The baby boy was pictured in his bassinet at the hospital with a football that Brook had signed. He was named Brook, according to his dad, "...after the two finest men I know, my dad and your son." I am so honored to have received that letter and picture.

I appreciate hearing from people. It's a great source of support to me in managing grief. Brook's birthday July 9th is a hard day for me, but I always look forward to hearing from Deb Avery of Humboldt, Nebraska, who shares that birth date with Brook. She sends me a note every year on Brook's birthday. I've learned to know her family, who've all grown up since I received her first letter.

I got to meet the lady who is in the "Because You Loved Me" video that was shown at the Spring game and at the funeral two days later. Her head was bandaged. She was taking Brook's hands when he visited at the hospital. She brought me a polaroid picture of the exact scene that is in the video.

I met lots of people that spent time with Brook when he was the team's ambassador his senior year. Lots of amusing stories–mostly having to do with hunting. One of the many stories I heard during the book tour is when Brook stopped at a farm to ask for hunting permission on their land. When they saw him at the door, they insisted on him coming in. The lady of the house was just taking an apple pie from the oven and he ate a piece of pie with them. Then they got out the camera and sat him down with the kids and took some pictures. Meanwhile, his two hunting buddies that were with him were sitting in the truck waiting for him so they could go hunting. They said the least he could have done was to bring them a piece of the pie.

I always say that I think that Brook had more hunting permission than anyone in the country. At least in the state of Nebraska. Tom Osborne says with a twinkle in his eye that if everyone really did hunt with Brook that said they did, Brook wouldn't have had time to go to classes or play football.

I got to meet the M & M boy and his family in Beatrice, Nebraska at a book signing. The story about the M & M boy is in *One Final Pass*. His mother showed me her son's M & M's. They were all carefully shellacked to preserve them. I was invited to be a speaker at an event in Beatrice and I was told that this family would be there. Prior to the event, I found a small double frame and took it to our Dependable Glass Company and explained my plan to Tom

Rohr. He made new glass covers on both sides so there would be space behind the glass like a shadowbox. He made one side so it would slide up and down. It was perfect for my plan. I "wall papered" it with Nebraska game snapshots, and put the wallet size '94 season's schedule with Brook's picture on the front, on one side and a picture from the inside flap of the book jacket on the other side. I put six shiny new M & M's in the side that slides. I could hardly wait until I went to Beatrice. I wrapped it up and took it with me and presented him with the gift. He opened it and I told him he can take those M & M's out and eat them and could put his shellacked M & M's in the shadowbox. He was delighted, as were his parents. Then they surprised me with a gift. It was a tall candy jar full of M & M's. I took it to school and every time one of my students got a 100 percent on their spelling test, including the bonus words, they could help themselves to a scoop of M & M's. It was on my desk at school and reminded me everyday of a great story about Brook and this boy.

Brook loved his two brittany hunting dogs, Juke, and his son, Bodie. Juke is buried at Plooster's place by the beautiful pond where the swan floats back and forth, where we had "Brook Berringer Day." He brought Bodie home the weekend before the accident. I thought as I observed Bodie's behavior the day of the accident that I was so glad he was here. At this overwhelming time, I wouldn't need to drive up to Lincoln to get him.

Close friends from Lincoln, Roger and Laura Saf, brought some of Brook's things to Goodland with them when they came after the accident. Laura hung Brook's hunting jacket on the back of a dining room chair. Bodie was pacing at the patio door, showing that he knew something was very wrong. I opened the door and let him in even though he was never in the house, and the house was full of people who'd just heard the news. He went straight to Brook's jacket and tugged one sleeve down until it draped onto the floor, then he lay down next to it and laid his head on it. He stayed there all day, not moving from his spot. Someone looked over at him later that day and said, "Whatcha gonna do with that dog?" I said, "You mean Bodie? Bodie Berringer?"

Bodie always knew the night before that pheasant season was starting the next day and he would be at the gate at 6:00 A.M. that next morning, howling. The gate was very near my next door neighbor Jay Herl's window. I would run to the door and make Bodie come and sit, then when I thought he was going to settle down, I'd go back to bed and he'd be right back to the gate, howling. I knew he was waking up their whole family. Jay runs a great Chevrolet dealership here and I bought my next vehicle from him. I was hoping it would help. And I've traded with him ever since. Great business. Great neighbors. Great friends.

Bodie eventually went to live with Chris and Stephanie Wilson, one of Brook's closest friends, near Joplin, Missouri. I knew he was lonely for Brook and missed hunting. Chris would take him hunting and do things with him.

For years, we emptied grass clippings from mowing in one corner of the back yard. We had a cat that taught Bodie to go to the grass clippings pile to do his business and bury it. You could look out and see grass clippings flying high into the air and know Bodie was there. I told Chris if he had a grass clippings pile, he'd never have to clean up after him in the yard. Chris said when he got back home from picking up Bodie and his really nice dog house that my brother-in-law, J. B. McClure made, Bodie made a bee-line from the truck to a pile of leaves in a corner of Chris's back yard. He said he doesn't have to clean up after him either.

I was concerned that he'd jump up on their little girl who was only four when Bodie came to live with Chris and his family. He was a big dog and he'd easily knock her down. Chris said the morning after he got back home with Bodie, they took their little girl outside to see him. He sat down, shaking, and wanting to jump all over everyone, but he sat there and looked at this little girl. She ran up to him, threw her arms around his neck, and said, "I love you, Bodilicious!" He was such a great dog and I know how much Brook loved him. I did, too. So did Chris and his family. He died recently at age 14.

The Games

My most memorable game was the Colorado game when Colorado was ranked No. 1 and Nebraska No. 2, and Brook was going to have his first starting job. He called me that week and told me not to listen to the news about the game. The news was saying Nebraska doesn't have a chance with that backup quarterback, what's-his-name? From-where-was-it? I knew Brook had heard a lot of it in spite of trying to ignore the media's predictions and just focus on playing. He had been preparing for each game as if he were the starter and I knew he was ready.

I listened to the pre-game commentators on the radio on the way to the game. They were broadcasting from the Nebraska bookstore. They were saying that every eye in the country is going to be on this game. One of them said, "Of all the players and all the coaches, I feel the most for Brook Berringer, who's starting today." The other one said, "Everybody is saying Nebraska doesn't have a chance with that backup quarterback, what's-his-name? From where-was-it?"and the other guy said, "Yeah, he's got to have the weight of the world on his shoulders for this game." They talked about his close relationship with his dad and how he missed him so much. They said, "We happen to have Brook's dad's twin brother, William Berringer, in here, and he agreed to visit with us." They talked with him about what Brook's dad was like. At the end of the segment, one said to the other, "Well, Brook's got a lot of pressure on him in this game," and the other one said, "Yeah, he sure does... and his dad has the best seat in the house."

Brook had a great game. We beat Colorado and were on the way to winning the National Championship. It was a very exciting game and I will never forget it. I took a picture of the greased goal posts before the game. They got torn down in spite of the very thick layer of grease on them.

Brook didn't set his goal to be the No. 2 quarterback at Nebraska and he did prepare for every game as if he were the starter. The '94 season gave him a chance to show what he could do. He kept the

Huskers on the way to the Orange Bowl, starting in the last seven games of the season. When they got to the Orange Bowl, Tommy Frazier was cleared to play again. The national media tried to engage Tom Osborne in a quarterback controversy. They kept pressuring him to declare who was going to start in the National Championship game. The half time that year was a huge circus act and they were practicing on the field. Tom Osborne finally told them that they'd probably have to start Brook as he's the only one tall enough to see out of those holes the elephants are making on the field.

Brook was disappointed that he didn't get to start in that game. The following year, his last one at Nebraska, proved to be as disappointing, but I'm proud of how he handled the situation. He lost his spot but not his contribution to the team. How a person plays the game shows something of his character. How he loses shows all of it.

Attendance at the funeral was a testament to the esteem for Brook that was held in the hearts of so many. It was held in the fieldhouse because it was the only place in Goodland that could seat that many people. A farmer in western Nebraska who later came to a book signing in his area quietly told me, "The day of the funeral? I couldn't get very good reception in the house so I went out to my tractor in the field and listened to the three hour service on my tractor radio." His eyes teared up as he said, "I'll never forget your son."

As the long caravan followed the hearse, many people were lined up along the road to the cemetery. I will never forget looking out of the window of the car and saw a man along the road who had on a red-for-Nebraska windbreaker. As we passed, he stood very still, took off his cap and held it across his heart. That image is etched permanently in my memory and it's one of the most touching things I've ever experienced. Remembering it always brings tears to my eyes.

There were so many other sincere tributes to my son. And they continue to arrive. So many people have told me they bought lots of copies of the book and use it to try to influence a young person's life, or a mother, or an athlete who is discouraged from working hard and not seeing great results, or someone struggling in the path around their own mountain.

When Kyle Orton was the quarterback at Purdue, the game announcers would tell the fans that Kyle wears #18 in honor of his role model, Brook Berringer. I knew that I had to meet him, so I called Nebraska's Sports Information Office to talk to the head honcho, Chris Anderson, who has become like a sister to me. I call her the Boss of Nebraska. She gave me contact information for the Sports Information Office at Purdue. I called and asked if he thought that Kyle Orton would be willing to visit for a short time with me. He assured me that he would most certainly be willing and he would set it up. So I drove from Western Kansas to Indianapolis to my sister and brother-in-law's, Jo and Stan. They went with me to Purdue and we met Kyle. It was wonderful to meet him.

Steve Ciphers from ESPN found out about it and did a segment on ESPN about the visit. He came to Goodland and interviewed me and took pictures of the Goodland Cowboys football field, announcing that this is where Brook played high school football as did his father before him. He interviewed Kyle and his parents. Kyle was asked about me coming to meet him and how that was. He said it was great. He thought we'd talk about ten or fifteen minutes and it was more like close to two hours and we didn't even mention football. I smiled when I watched the segment and said, "No kidding? We didn't even mention football? I guess we didn't." His dad said he was in eighth grade I believe, at the time of Brook's accident, and that he was devastated. He said when he struggled with adversity as an athlete, he would stop and ask himself, "What would Brook do?"

As I reflect on these fifteen years since Brook's passing, I have a whirlwind of thoughts. I think about how God has been showing me the way down the path around my mountain. I think of the verse about the footprints in the sand. When there's two sets of footprints, God is walking beside me. When you only see one set, God has been carrying me. My strength comes from my Heavenly Father. My faith has never been more important to me. Without God, this journey would be insurmountable. I also think about how God has blessed me with the strength and courage of my dad. All the people I've met, all the great stories I've heard, having a close relationship with Coach Osborne, Ron Brown, and Turner Gill and their families, and with Mark Miller, Hobie and the rest of the Sawyer Brown group all come to mind as some of the many blessings I hold dearly. My daughters and sons-in-law and my incredible grandchildren are my most precious gift. And the greatest blessing of all is knowing that my son is with his Heavenly Father and his earthly father. The best gift anyone can give to those they love, is the assurance when they leave this life, they will be in eternity with our Lord forever.

Wishing you God's richest blessings.
Jan

REFLECTIONS ON BROOK

Too often in this misguided world, glowing words are heaped on an individual to the point of idolization. Unfortunately, there are some who bask in such glory and eagerly ask for even more. That was not Brook Berringer. Brook demonstrated humility, among many other positive traits. No one can tell what he might have accomplished in an NFL career, which would now have been at its conclusion. But one thing is for certain. Since his untimely death fifteen years ago, countless thousands have been beneficiaries of his spiritual legacy. This has resulted in an acknowledgement of gratitude and esteem for the bright personality he displayed.

Though he was more than just a football quarterback, his coaches certainly knew him significantly in that respect. Tom Osborne, now the Athletic Director for the University of Nebraska at Lincoln—after a stint in the United States Congress—was head coach for the Cornhuskers during all of the five years Brook was on the team.

He stated: "Sometimes when a young person dies, it is a common response to mention all of that young person's virtues while ignoring the negatives. As a result, the person is often portrayed as being perfect and this picture is not really accurate. In Brook's case, all of the accolades and nice things that were said about him were accurate and there really wasn't anything that those of us who knew him could say that had negative connotations.

"Brook had a great love of life. He was busy exploring many

interests every day. He loved outdoor activities and was an avid hunter and fisherman. He loved flying. He loved football and he cared about his family. He didn't have a mean bone in his body. I never heard him say anything critical about another person. He was too busy doing the things that he enjoyed.

"I was serving as the quarterback coach so I was in all the quarterback meetings, which lasted from 30-45 minutes every day before our team meetings, and I worked with him a great deal on the field. As a result, over the period of his five years at Nebraska, I spent as much time with Brook as anyone on our team and got to know him fairly well. We shared a love of outdoor activities and we would often talk about his hunting and fishing adventures. He even asked me one time if he could hunt on some property that I owned near Lincoln and later came back with a picture of a coyote that he had called in and shot while hunting on the property.

"Brook was very much the kind of person you would want to be part of your family or someone that you would want your daughter to marry. I sensed that during his time here at Nebraska, he grew spiritually. He came from a Christian home, having lost his dad when he was only six or seven years of age to cancer. His mother was a person of strong faith and raised him with Christian values and principles. Like many young people, Brook was probably living out a faith that was mostly inherited from his family. However, as time went on, he matured in his own beliefs and became a committed Christian while he was here. He lived out his faith in the way he treated other people and in the way that he played football.

"Brook had exceptional courage. During the 1994 season after Tommie Frazier was lost for most of the year with blood clots in his leg, Brook played through two deflated lung injuries and held our team together and took us to a national championship. As I have chronicled in other places, Brook's greatest contribution to our football team came not in 1994 when he led us to the national championship, but rather in 1995 when Tommie Frazier returned to action and eventually won the starting quarterback job back from Brook. Brook could have been cynical, could have quit, could have led a revolt, but he spoke volumes to me and to his teammates in the way that he responded. He was very supportive of Tommie Frazier, he played his role perfectly and even though he was not on the field as much as he liked, he was a big part of our success during the 1995 season.

"His loss in a plane crash a couple of months after the season ended was devastating to me and to the rest of the team. I think most young people feel that they are somewhat invincible and the death of a teammate always hits hard and reminds other team members of their own mortality. I know that a great many players reexamined their spiritual lives after Brook's crash. They saw how powerful his example had been to not only teammates, but to thousands of fans in Nebraska and Kansas. They realized that even though Brook's life was relatively short, his impact had been huge and also they realized that he had made the most of 22+ years in the way that he had lived his life and committed his life to Christ. I personally felt very much as though I had lost a member of my own family when Brook died and can remember standing in the Stadium at the spring game with tears in my eyes as a video was played of Brook.

"Brook's life is a true testimony of the difference that one person can make. Often times that difference is made in unexpected ways but it has a ripple effect on many lives across the generations. I will always remember Brook as someone who was truly unique and someone who made quite probably the greatest impact for good of any player that I have coached."

Nebraska fans are reminded continually of the link between Tom Osborne and Brook Berringer whenever they approach the north entrance of Memorial Stadium. A life-sized bronze statue has stood there since 2006 as a lasting tribute to the surpassing quality of both men.

Another coach of significance in Brook Berringer's life was Turner Gill, his position coach at the time and now the head football coach at the University of Kansas.

Brook respected Turner, not only because he was his coach, but also because he had previously proved himself as one of the greatest quarterbacks in Cornhusker history–coming within an eyelash of a national championship of his own in 1983.

In reflecting on his relationship with the player, Turner observed, "Brook Berringer had several physical qualities that a coach looks for in a quarterback. He was an excellent passer in terms of both strength and accuracy. He was a great draft prospect for the NFL, where his skills were a better fit than at Nebraska where we ran the option. He played well for Nebraska, but he was made for the NFL.

"The things that stood out for Brook went way beyond his physical qualities and outstanding people skills. He was hard working, dependable, reliable; characteristics as great as you can say about an athlete or quarterback. He was able to elevate his personal attributes and was one of the reasons why Nebraska had National Championships in 1994 and 1995.

"Throughout Brook's time at Nebraska, I think people would say there were many who saw him as the leader he was. Brook was unselfish and he put the needs of the team ahead of his own opportunities when they arose, so that whether he was the starter or not, he still had great influence. When he talked, people listened.

"I was proud to be Brook's coach and his friend. I count among my greatest memories the time he came in and told me he had given his life to Christ. I look forward to being with him again in Heaven."

Though he was not a coach, Chris Bahl as Director of Licensing was very much involved in the Athletic Department at UNL. Bahl developed Husker Authentics, which delivers quality athletic gear to fans from the store near Memorial Stadium. He and Brook developed a close relationship because of their love of sports and especially fishing. His recollections of Brook are worth hearing.

"I will never forget April 18, 1996, for the rest of my life. It was a gorgeous spring day, sun shining and a warm wind blowing. It was an exciting time at work as the Huskers had just won their second consecutive football national championship. It was the week of the spring game as well as the NFL Draft. The atmosphere around

Nebraska Football was never greater. I saw Brook that day, as he and his friend Toby Lake were headed out of the West Stadium for an afternoon of flying. I had a short conversation with Brook and wished him the best in the draft. Brook smiled, shrugged and said, "Bahl, it's all in God's hands." I will never forget that statement. We laughed, patted each other on the shoulder and departed . . . it's still all in slow motion in my mind. Why didn't I hug Brook? Why didn't I tell him how much I respected him? I could have said, 'I love you.' None of us will ever know why things happen the way they do . . . we just have to have faith and find peace that it's all in God's hands.

"Hours later when I heard of Brook's accident I was in disbelief and denial. I dialed Coach Osborne and then hung up . . . I didn't want to know. That night I struggled with the thought of going to the FCA Banquet at the Bob Devaney Sports Center. I was hurt badly. I prayed. I cried. Time passed slowly as if in a blur. When I walked onto the floor of the Sports Center I first saw the "Influence" portraits lined up on the stage, which were to be gifts for the athletes who were to speak. This had been arranged weeks before. I was sobbing when I saw the little boy in the "18" jersey in the portrait. I couldn't believe my eyes. It was then that I felt Brook's presence and peace. While it was undoubtedly a very sad day, it was starting to take on the feeling that something was happening that was much bigger than any of us, football or our world."

Chris's further reflections on the team bus trip to Kansas and the emotions of the funeral service for Brook reflect the thoughts of hundreds who were there.

"On Aril 22, 1996, I boarded a bus outside of the South Stadium for a journey back to Kansas. I dreaded the thought of going back to Goodland to say 'good bye' to such a good friend. I took a seat next to Chad Stanley, who besides playing football was also a hunting and fishing buddy of Brook's. On the trip down we shared hunting stories, looked for turkeys and talked fishing. As we exited the bus in Goodland, the first person I recognized was my high school coach, Rocky Welton. Rocky had coached at Goodland before moving to my hometown of Garden City. He had coached Brook and was close to the Berringers. Brook and I had often exchanged 'Rocky stories.' There was never a coach I was closer to than Rocky. His expression communicated that he was glad to see me and we hugged as neither of us said a word. As we walked into the Max Jones Fieldhouse for the funeral service I told Chad that I felt Brook's presence. He nodded and agreed. It took everything I had to not lose it when I saw Brook's casket, with his helmet resting on top of it. On the stage, I saw a group of men I was close to and each of who knew me differently. There was Coach Osborne, Ron Brown, Turner Gill, Art Lindsay, and Rocky Welton; dear friends who have impacted my own life in different ways. I began to wonder about myself.

"Rocky knew me as a cocky, mouthy, confident fighter with a big heart and a deep desire for sports–the kind of kid Rocky liked.

"Tom knew me as a young go-getter with an entrepreneurial spirit who loved to fish. He and I would much rather talk about fishing than anything else in our lives when we were together.

"Art knew me as a young aggressive sport professional with a big heart and lots of questions about the meaning of life. As the service went on and I listened intently to each speaker talk about Brook, life, and our Savior, my head spun with deep questions about myself. I don't believe I was being selfish–I truly believe Brook was there, pushing me to think about where I was in my own life. I remember thinking, 'What if I had died instead of Brook? Where was I headed?'

"I have never felt more in tune with faith than I did that day. As Art Lindsay began his eulogy I heard his voice shoot through my head like a bolt of lightening with 2 Corinthians 5:17. This verse was on my list of verses to memorize from Art as he and I met weekly. As we left the fieldhouse at Goodland High School I looked back and knew my life was changed forever.

"Still to this day I have Brook in my heart and on my mind, especially when I am coaching and parenting. Our conversations were always around the outdoors first, then football and then life. I knew Brook was meeting with our mutual friend Art Lindsay.

"I saw firsthand how tough Brook was at halftime of the Wyoming game when he broke several ribs and collapsed a lung. He knew the situation of the team and was not about to let the guys down. I remember putting my hand on his pads and telling him how much I admired him. It was a moment that took my breath away as well as those around him that day. Brook Berringer had many of those moments. A quote from Leo Buscaglia I share with each one of my teams I coach today reminds me of Brook–'Your talent is God's gift to you. What you do with it is your gift back to God.'"

Today Chris and his wife Julie are parents of four beautiful kids, all of whom are very active in sports. He has had several positions since leaving Nebraska. Now in addition to his business activities he coaches kids teams in football, wrestling and baseball.

"During these last 15 years," he affirms, "I made a full commitment to be involved in my children's lives. I also made the commitment to use their interest in sports as a platform to teach them the Word of the Lord as well as show them how to share their own faith. When I coach, I always wear a baseball cap labeled with a red '18' under the bill. The kids I have coached know why I use number '18' because I have shared the story of Brook Berringer with just about all of them. The story I tell about Brook is not one of tragedy, but rather one of the ultimate competitor and teammate. They always ask, 'Coach, what happened to Brook?' My response is always the same, 'Brook was Drafted #1 on April 18, 1996.'

"The time I spent at Nebraska is the foundation for who I am today. It was truly a special time. While football was the platform that brought us all together, it was faith that bonded us. The relationships I developed during my time in Nebraska will impact generations of my own family. Men like Tom Osborne, Art Lindsay, Ron Brown, Chris Bubak and Brook Berringer have impacted my life forever. Being an outdoorsman I refer to such men of God as 'Life Guides.' Everyday I aspire to be a 'Life Guide' and do the best I can to be as much an inspiration to others as these men were to me.

"I also often think of Jan Berringer and pray for her. Her life almost mirrors in many ways Brook's time at Nebraska. She, too, has had to persevere. Jan has worked hard and raised a beautiful family. Brook was a model of that effort.

Chris Bubak, to whom Bahl referred was the Lincoln Area Representative for the Fellowship of Christian Athletes while Brook played football at Nebraska. He is now the State Director for FCA. He recalled, "It was the summer of 1995 the first time I met with Brook in the Hewit Center where the academic center and training table were located. He and his girlfriend were meeting me to talk about getting involved in a summer study so they could learn more about what the Bible says about the person and work of Jesus Christ.

"I was looking forward to meeting Brook because we had a lot in common. His hometown was not too far from where I grew up and we both shared a love for hunting and flying. I also had a sense that God was working in Brook's heart so that he could see his need for a Savior.

"In the spring of 1996, I saw Brook for the last time in this life. It was again in the Hewit Center and he was leaving to go flying with his friend Tobey. This time we talked about his opportunity to share his relationship with Jesus Christ publicly for the first time to over 800 people at the Lincoln FCA banquet later that evening. God had done an amazing work in Brook's life and he was willing to tell the whole world about it.

"The Apostle Paul wrote, 'For our sake he made him to be sin who knew no sin, so that in him we might become the righteousness of God (2 Corinthians 5:21).' I think this verse best describes what God did in Brook's life. God had opened Brook's eyes to see he had been living in rebellion to God and His perfect holy standard. By God's grace, Brook then came to understand the message of the cross; that Jesus had taken on Brook's sin and had given in return 'the righteousness of God in Him.'

"Many people think it's only bad people who need the gospel, but when good people like Brook repent–it's also a miracle. Christianity is not about becoming good, or cleaning up one's life.

Jesus didn't need to die to save anyone from an immoral lifestyle. You can clean up your life without him. People do it all the time. Besides, if good is the aim of the Gospel then from what do 'good' people repent? Obviously, conversion brings a change, but salvation is not about the adjustment of one's behavior from bad to good. Christianity is not about our "goodness" at all. It is about Jesus' "goodness." Jesus' righteousness makes the goodness of the best people look like a dung heap by comparison (Philippians 3:8-10).'

"Brook had responded to that message by confessing his sin to God and agreeing with God that he was a sinner deserving of God's punishment of sin. He had also repented of his sin and had begun to live a new life that had started to look more and more like the life of Christ. That was the message he had wanted to share with the FCA crowd that night.

"While we grieved his death, our grief was mingled with the hope we have in Christ that the dead shall rise and we will all be caught up together with them in Christ (1 Thessalonians 4:13-18)."

TRIBUTES WORTHY OF THE MAN

Brook Berringer had a capacity for compassion far greater than most ever attain. He exemplified so perfectly what it was to fulfill the instruction of Jesus in Matthew 5:29 to "turn the other cheek." He took every slap that came his way, even deep wounds of the spirit, and regenerated them into kindness for others. And to him that was no big deal. That's the way he learned to live life from his father and mother. He didn't go around looking for recognition, in fact he often shied away from it. His concept of life boiled down to a very simple formula. He expounded, "Doing things for others is not a sacrifice, it is one of the true joys of life."

One of the gifts he received for Valentine's Day, February 14, 1996, was the classic by Oswald Chambers, *My Utmost for His Highest*. He began to read the daily lesson the first thing every morning. On March 13–shortly after putting down his hunting partner Juke–he came to a familiar scripture verse: John 3:16. His eyes brightened as he personally identified with two key sentences Chambers wrote in the passage: "Beware of talking about abandonment if you know nothing about it, and you will never know anything about it until you have realized that John 3:16 means that God gave himself absolutely. In our abandonment we give ourselves over to God just as God gave Himself for us, without any calculation."

As Brook closed the book that morning, Oswald Chambers'

incisive thought about abandonment was the prayer of his heart. "That's what I want," he determined.

That commitment, done so privately in his heart, was so apparent on the outside to everyone who knew him. It's obvious that in his pursuit of God, Brook Berringer accomplished more in his brief run through life than most ever even dream.

It is little wonder that the news of his death and subsequent details of his life were consumed by the public and led to a reaction of adulation and praise. The Berringer family received more than 10,000 letters, cards, and notes of sympathy and encouragement. Apart from those messages, surely the most poetic observation of all was written by Jim Rose, former University of Nebraska sportscaster, "Whenever I see something that reminds me of Brook … a college kid holding a child's hand or signing an autograph, smiling for a photo or a loving embrace with his mom or dad, I'm reminded of what Shakespeare's Juliet cried of her lost Romeo: 'Death lies upon him like a frost upon the prettiest flower in all the field.'"

Within six months of the time that flower fell, the first edition of *One Final Pass* was published and quickly sold more than 60,000 copies–making it a best seller. Not only his adoring fans, but also thousands who knew little about him were enthralled with the clear testimony of a life lived to the fullest. Yet, at the same time, there was a prevailing sadness that such a life of promise had been cut far too short.

One of the most unusual results of the book's publication was a domino effect on a 16-year-old student from Pierce, Nebraska. In a thank you note she wrote. "I finally accepted the Lord Jesus as my personal Savior. If not for the book, *One Final Pass* I don't think it would have happened. The proceeds from the book provided my scholarship money to attend the Fellowship of Christian Athlete's summer camp. I am really shy and tend to back away when afraid. So when my friend approached me about going to camp I thought I could say 'yes' and then back out later. But when I got everything paid for and my friend did also, I couldn't back out. Because of this camp, I found the Lord and am never turning back again."

A similar response came from a teenager in Stromsburg, Nebraska: "FCA camp was an awesome experience for me. I attended a session on how to share Christ without fear. I learned a lot at that session and on my way home I was able to witness to four people. Once home I was given the chance to share my experience at my church. Many were touched and took my words to heart. They were inspired that at my young age (17). I had so much faith in the Lord. So they too went out into the world and witnessed to others.

"The experience has changed my life and now I am not afraid to show others my faith. I know that God wants me to go to FCA Camp again next year to have another mountaintop experience."

It is fascinating that the lure of the book reached beyond those who are sports-minded. One such Lincoln woman, aware of who Brook was, joined in a contest with her husband to see who could finish reading the book first. On a business trip to Florida, since she was the one working, he readily completed the story. So she was left to finish it on the plane ride home. "At 35,000 feet in the air," she testified, "the Holy Spirit grabbed and tugged at my heart and hasn't let go since."

She had grown up in church and had gone to a parochial school but as an adult she started escaping church by going to the Village Inn for breakfast. "I knew about the Jesus story," she said. "I just wasn't always interested in the rituals of going to church and living my life by His example. But when we had our two children, my life began to change. I had a desire for them to have something to build their lives on and felt obligated to bring them up in the faith. Through their learning about Jesus and seeing my husband do his devotions every day, I was starting to have a desire stir within me. But pride stopped me dead in my tracks from speaking about it and I was secretly dying inside, dying to have the understanding and relationship that I saw in others.

"So as I was finishing up *One Final Pass*, I was touched by

Brook's life. But it was in his death and the words spoken by Ron Brown at the FCA banquet that first got my attention. Ron spoke about the time he was on a track team in New York and how two men off the street jumped in and competed, finishing first and second. But their names weren't listed in the newspaper because they didn't belong to the team. I took that story personally. I thought he was asking me if I had made my declaration of whose team I was on. Of course, I had not done so publicly. Deep in my heart I knew I loved Jesus, but that's about all I had been ready to acknowledge.

"As tears were starting to well up in my eyes, I continued reading. I can still remember the feeling of my heart starting to pump faster and faster, as if I was running the race right then. The final blow came as I reached the ending pages of the Epilogue. Chris Bahl from the Nebraska Athletic Department was sharing about his relationship with Brook and the effect that Brook's death had on him. His life was filled with a 'deep yearning in his heart to be a man of God' and how he 'felt like an outsider, wanting to get in.' That was me! Chris was describing me. Tears and uncontrollable sobs came pouring out of my body as I was sitting on the plane, feeling close to heaven. Chris later described himself as a 'closet Christian.' And that's who I was. I was hiding the desires of my heart about Jesus from my husband, my children, my family and most importantly from God Himself.

"Since I was such a mess, with tears flowing and sounds of sniffling, I couldn't hide what was happening. My husband questioned me about the sudden outpouring of emotions but I couldn't answer him. I just sat there and sobbed uncontrollably. When I finally gained my composure, I was able to share what had happened and declared to God and to my husband that I wasn't going to be a 'closet Christian' anymore. I knew I was a sinner and needed to confess aloud my commitment to Christ and to begin a living relationship with the One who died for me. Since that moment my life has been an extraordinary journey."

An acquaintance from Goodland, Kansas, became aware of

the assurance that Brook walked with when he read *One Final Pass*. In the years before that, whenever Brook was home from college, they played together on the town basketball team. "Brook was a very likable person," he wrote, "but looking back, I would never dream of the impact his short but powerful life would have on so many.

"The day I went to the funeral, I never had a clue that a 'revival' was actually going to take place. That was an awesome funeral. The truth was so clearly spoken. Everyone that was present definitely had a seed planted in his or her hearts. A testimony showed by the influence talked about in the book. I've never been a big fan of funerals, but I'm thankful that many members of my family were present. I was pleasantly surprised that Brook had accepted Christ–his life touching so many people in such a short time.

"Many times, I have reflected on the funeral service held in that fieldhouse, celebrating not the deaths that happened, but the number of lives that have been saved by the results of that service. It was such an incredible moment to hear the words of those who love the Lord spoken in a public building."

A couple of years after that, a man in Omaha was impacted by reading *One Final Pass*. "Less than 10 days after Brook accepted Jesus Christ as his Lord and Savior [that would be early September 1994] I had a CT Scan for what I thought was kidney stones. Needless to say I was shocked to hear that I had a Stage III tumor on one kidney. They removed the kidney and a few other things on Labor Day. It was touch and go for 19 days.

"For the past few years I had felt an emptiness. It is hard to explain, but I knew something was needed to give my life balance. I suspected it was God, but I was bullheaded and would not open up and accept Him."

More than a year passed, when in November 1995, he wrote, "The curtain opened, the light went on, my eyes opened! What I was missing in my life was God!! All I had to do was accept that fact! So simple, yet so hard. On Easter 1996, I was baptized. I cannot begin to tell how I felt–the weight of the world lifted off my shoulder. And it was God doing the lifting. The best day of my life was when I accepted Jesus!

"I saw myself in many passages of the wonderful testament to Brook's life and God. As a matter of fact, the first prayer I've ever initiated and said with my family was right after we heard the news about Brook's death. My wife, son, and I joined hands, kneeled on the family room floor, and prayed to God to accept Brook into His arms."

A freshman at Seward High School in Nebraska had a similar, albeit less traumatic experience after reading the book. "It's the most beautiful book I have ever read. It showed me what a wonderful person Brook Berringer was. I never knew him. I'd never seen him anywhere but on TV and yet I felt like I knew him for years. Just from reading his story, he's become one of my biggest role models. I want to be just like him! I have already accepted Jesus Christ as my Savior and given my life to God.

"As I read the book, it kept inspiring me more and more to be like Brook and be able to give as freely as he did. In the last few chapters, I couldn't help from crying and wishing I could have known Brook better while he was still alive. But at the same time I was crying tears of joy because Brook was such a beautiful person and he deserved to be in heaven with both of his fathers.

"As an athlete, I can relate to Brook. I've always been one of the 'star' players, playing the whole game. This year I was lucky enough to make the JV basketball team as a freshman. Reading this book has really helped me to become more of a team player. It has also helped me to work hard to be the best I can be, not only on the court but off the court as well."

An Iowa girl, who was a huge Cornhusker fan, in reading *One Final Pass* was finally able to bring closure to the death of a close friend. "When I think of Brook's life and of the Bible verses throughout the book, it really touches me. Sometimes a small tear slowly makes its way down my cheek. Those verses remind me of a friend who loved football. He passed away this year at the young age of 14. I wonder if he and Brook play football together in heaven."

Not everyone who read the story of Brook Berringer was in a state of despair. One University of Nebraska senior was on the top of her world. She had attained every goal she had set for herself since junior high and she credited God for her successes, Her favorite Bible verse was Philippians 4:13: "I can do all things through Christ who strengthens me." Her success in sports and academics followed her to UNL where she maintained a 3.9 GPA in engineering. In addition to a long list of social accomplishments, she was named Homecoming Queen during her senior year. She said, "The Lord blessed me in every way possible. Yet for some reason for the past year, I have felt distant from Him. I felt so empty inside even though I have the world in the palm of my hands.

"You see, every goal I had set has been achieved. Every dream has come true–except what really matters in my spiritual life. But thanks to reading *One Final Pass*, I want information on FCA and a Bible study group of young adults like me!

A Lincoln businessman had met Brook in the summer of 1994 when several NU athletes visited his place of business. He talked with Brook about their shared interest in upland bird hunting and hoped to hunt together that fall. "But it didn't work out due to his injury and busy schedule. He seemed wise beyond his years. He was down to earth and humble unlike some college athletes. My son and I were getting ready to attend our first FCA Spring Banquet when we heard the tragic news of Brook's death.

"As soon as I heard about *One Final Pass*, I immediately bought a copy and devoured it in one night. I couldn't put it down. It was a huge turning point in my Christian walk. Through a neighborhood Bible Study, my wife's heart and mine were opened to God's Word. Brook's story was like a lightning bolt that connected everything for me. For over 40 years I had thought I was a good Christian without really understanding that salvation was a gift, something that I didn't have to earn. The co-leader of our Bible Study led me to place my faith in Jesus. About a week later, I attended the FCA Friday Bible Study where the author of the book also attends."

The University of Nebraska Athletic Department has also done its share in honoring the memory of Brook Berringer. A year after his death, the Brook Berringer Citizenship Team was established in his honor. It recognizes the fact that he was one of the most dedicated Husker volunteers in the community. The team honors players who exhibit similar commitment for volunteering in the community. Honorees must have a minimum 2.5 cumulative GPA, completed at least eight new service activities in the past year, and have had no off-field incidents.

More than one hundred football players have been named to the Citizenship Team since it was established. The squad members are recognized at the Red-White Spring game.

A second prestigious award was established in 1997 as the result of a Sawyer Brown Benefit Concert in August. The proceeds from the event were used to fund the Brook Berringer Memorial Endowed Scholarship. Each year, a deserving athlete receives a fullride college scholarship. Criteria for the award include the following: must be a football student-athlete, must be involved in community service along with high ideals, excellent character and integrity. The player and his parents are part of an on-field presentation before the start of the first home game each season. Brook's mother Jan and other members of the Berringer family are also part of the presentation.

BROOK BERRINGER CITIZENSHIP TEAM

1996

Established in honor of the late Nebraska quarterback who died in plane crash in April 1995, the Brook Berringer Citizenship Team annually honors Nebraska Football players who have consistently went above and beyond the call of duty providing excellent leadership, involvement and service.

Honorees must have a minimum 2.5 cumulative GPA, completed at least eight new service activities in the past year and have had no off-field incidents.

The recipients of the award are announced and honored on the field at Nebraska football's annual Spring Game.

2011 Brook Berringer Citizenship Team

Rex Burkhead, Mike Caputo, Brion Carnes, Austin Cassidy, Ben Cotton, Jared Crick, Jim Ebke, Tyler Evans, Cody Green, Thomas Grove, Alex Henery, Marcel Jones, Tyler Legate, Mathew May, Colin McDermott, Marcus Mendoza, Courtney Osborne, Steven Osborne, Kevin Thomsen, Lance Thorell, Donovan Vestal, C.J. Zimmerer

2010 Brook Berringer Citizenship Team

Prince Amukamara, Anthony Blue, Rex Burkhead, Ben Cotton, Jared Crick, Cody Green, Thomas Grove, Michael Hays, Alex Henery, Will Henry, Austin Jones, D.J. Jones, Marcel Jones, Blake LawrenceZac Lee, Marcus Mendoza, Kyler Reed, Lance Thorell

2009 Brook Berringer Citizenship Team
Jake Wesch, Tyler Wortman, Todd Peterson, Marcel Jones, Dan Glassman, Alex Henery, Marcus Mendoza, Adi Kunalic, Dan Titchener, Anthony Blue, Blake Lawrence, Lance Thorell

2008 Brook Berringer Citizenship Team
Joe Ganz, Aaron Gillaspie, Cody Glenn, Victory Haines, Blake Lawrence, T.J. O'Leary, Todd Peterson, Matt Senske, Dan Titchener, Jake Wesch, Tyler Wortman

2007 Brook Berringer Citizenship Team
Greg Austin, Titus Brothers, Victory Haines, Will Henry, Todd Peterson, J.B. Phillips, Brandon Rigoni, Matt Senske, Dan Titchener, Jake Wesch

2006 Brook Berringer Citizenship Team
2006 Team Members: Greg Austin, Cortney Grixby, Brandon Jackson, Brandon Koch, Eric Lueshen, Kurt Mann, Matt Senske, Zac Taylor, Dan Titchener, Dane Todd, Jake Wesch

2005 Brook Berringer Citizenship Team
Willie Amos, Greg Austin, Joe Dailey, Sandro DeAngelis, Garth Glissman, Mark LeFlore, Eric Lueshen, Kurt Mann, Jeff McBride, Jake Peetz, Dane Todd, Jake Wesch, Ben Zajicek

2004 Brook Berringer Citizenship Team
Titus Adams, Willie Amos, Joe Dailey, Sandro DeAngelis, Garth Glissman, Steve Kriewald, Jeff McBride, Mike McLaughlin, Ryan Ommert, Jake Peetz, Chad Sievers, Dane Todd, Ben Zajicek

2003 Brook Berringer Citizenship Team
Demoine Adams, Will Dabbert, Sandro DeAngelis, M.J. Flaum, Garth Glissman, Troy Hassebroek, Steve Kriewald, Jack Limbaugh, Mike McLaughlin, Ryan Ommert, Josh Sewell, Dane Todd, Tyler Toline, Curt Tomasevicz, Ben Zajicek; Honorable-Mention: Adam

Hassebroek, Brandon Koch, Jeff McBride, Alex Shada, Kyle Ringenberg

2002 Brook Berringer Citizenship Team
Willie Amos, Will Dabbert, Judd Davies, Joe Chrisman, Sandro DeAngelis, Troy Hassebroek, Patrick Kabongo, Chris Kelsay, David Kolowski, Steve Kriewald, Jack Limbaugh, Mike McLaughlin, Ryan Ommert, Phil Peetz, Pat Ricketts, Kyle Ringenberg

2001 Brook Berringer Citizenship Team
Demoine Adams, Dan Alexander, Willie Amos, Rod Baker, Will Dabbert, Troy Hassebroek, Jeff Hemje, Patrick Kabongo, Jack Limbaugh, Jake McKee, Jon Penny, Ryan Ommert

2000 Brook Berringer Citizenship Team
Dan Alexander, Rod Baker, Will Dabbert, Jeff Hemje, Jake McKee, Willie Miller, Bobby Newcombe, Jon Penny, Jason Schwab, Brian Shaw

1999 Brook Berringer Citizenship Team
Dan Alexander, Rod Baker, Matt Baldwin, Will Dabbert, Matt Davison, Jeff Hemje, Jake McKee, Bobby Newcombe, Jon Penny, Brian Shaw; Lifetime Achievement Award: Bill Doleman

1998 Brook Berringer Citizenship Team
Dan Alexander, Kris Brown, Matt Davison, Demond Finister, Jeff Hemje, Sheldon Jackson, Chad Kelsay, Brian Shaw, James Sherman; Lifetime Acheivement Award: Tom Osborne

1997 Brook Berringer Citizenship Team
Dan Alexander, Rod Baker, Demond Finister, Kris Brown, Ahman Green, Brandt Wade, Brendan Zahl, Jared Tomich, Grant Wistrom; Honorary Member: Trev Alberts